Spiritual Leadership

Spiritual Leadership

KINGDOM FOUNDATION PRINCIPLES

SECOND EDITION

Bill Vincent

RWG Publishing

CONTENTS

About The Author

Recommended Books

RWG Publishing

PO Box 596

Litchfield, IL 62056

https://rwgpublishing.com/

Published in the United States of America

Paperback: 978-1-79476-131-5

1

✎

Arm Yourself

All across the world Christian people have not truly learned the ability to arm themselves. A Christian who is not prepared to suffer is comparable to a soldier who goes to war unarmed.

1 Peter 4:1 Forasmuch then as Christ hath suffered for us in the flesh, arm yourselves likewise with the same mind: for he that hath suffered in the flesh hath ceased from sin;

Just as a human being matures physically and mentally, a believer also matures spiritually. We begin our spiritual walk with Christ as babies (1 Peter 2:2) and ideally progress from infancy to childhood and then to adulthood or maturity (Ephesians 4:14; Hebrews 5:14).

Physical growth progresses with the passage of time. You will never find a two-year-old who is six feet tall! You cannot hurry physical maturity because it is a function of time. You naturally grow at a predetermined rate that is tied to the passage of time.

Intelligent growth is not a function of time but of learning. If you are thirty years old and have yet to master the first-grade level of reading, you will not be able to comprehend the tenth-grade level. Conversely, there are twelve-year-olds who have completed their high school education.

Spiritual growth is not a function of time or learning. I am sorry to report there are people who have been saved for years who are still immature babies or children in the spirit. This even includes people well-versed in Scriptures and memorization. Their knowledge of the Word does not mean they are skilled in its application.

If spiritual growth was a function of learning scripture, the Pharisees would have been the most mature of Jesus' day. They could quote the first five books of the Bible from memory, yet they didn't recognize the Son of God as He cast out demons and raised the dead.

So what causes spiritual growth? We just read that those who suffer as Christ suffered have reached spiritual maturity. Is it a function of suffering? I know many who have suffered greatly in their Christian walk, yet they remain in the trenches of bitterness and despair. These are not the spiritually mature. Suffering in itself does not cause spiritual growth. Maturity is found through our obedience to God in the midst of suffering. This is what it means to suffer as Christ suffered.

Hebrews 5:8 Though he were a Son, yet learned he obedience by the things which he suffered;

The suffering Jesus experienced was the direct result of His obedience to the will of God. The course or flow of this world's system directly opposes the kingdom of God; therefore, when we obey God we move against the current. This automatically introduces conflict, which gives birth to persecution, affliction, and tribulation. Obedience in the midst of this conflict causes spiritual growth. Examine again the words of Peter.

1 Peter 4:1, 2 Forasmuch then as Christ hath suffered for us in the flesh, arm yourselves likewise with the same mind: for he that hath suffered in the flesh hath ceased from sin; That he no longer should live the rest of *his* time in the flesh to the lusts of men, but to the will of God.

Suffering after the pattern of Christ brings a believer to maturity. This kind of suffering is caused when we resist the will of man to submit to the will of God.

It is not the religious suffering of self-induced pain and neglect. It is not dying of a disease or lacking the finances to pay your bills. God receives no glory from these. This mentality has actually caused many to search for an opportunity to inflict themselves with suffering in order to feel worthy. They believe God is pleased if they make themselves suffer for

Him. This perverts their relationship, causing it to be based on works and not grace.

We are to embrace the suffering Christ experienced. Jesus did not suffer because He was diseased and lacked money to pay His bills.

No, the suffering He experienced was to be tempted in every manner possible and yet remain obedient to His Father. He was "in all points tempted as we are, yet without sin" (Hebrews 4:15).

We face resistance when our desire and the desire of those who influence our will to go one direction, but God wills another.

Jesus and His disciples had come into the region of Caesarea Philippi. He questioned them as to who they thought He was. In answer, Peter boldly declared Jesus to be the Christ, the Son of the living God. Jesus affirmed Peter's revelation.

Immediately following this, Jesus told them He was going to Jerusalem, would suffer many things, be killed, and then rise again. This disturbed Peter, so he pulled Jesus aside and rebuked Him.

Matthew 16:23 But he turned, and said unto Peter, Get thee behind me, Satan: thou art an offence unto me: for thou savourest not the things that be of God, but those that be of men.

Jesus had told His disciples that it was God's will that He suffer, die, and rise again. Yet Peter and the other disciples believed it was only a matter of time before Jesus set up His kingdom (Acts 1:6). They had all endured so much hardship to follow Jesus. Why would He die now when the hope of the kingdom was so near?

Peter was confused. *What does He mean, "I am going to die"? What will happen to us? What good could His dying possibly do?*

His fears focused on self-preservation instead of the will of the Father. He had yielded to the desires of the same selfish nature that entered man at the fall. It is the self-ruled will that opposes the will of God. Jesus seized the opportunity and used Peter's error to teach the disciples this powerful truth:

Matthew 16:24. 25 Then said Jesus unto his disciples, If any *man* will come after me, let him deny himself, and take up his cross, and follow me.

For whosoever will save his life shall lose it: and whosoever will lose his life for my sake shall find it. The only way to walk with Jesus is to completely deny yourself and take up the cross. This means dying to your own desire and will. This attitude enables you to follow Christ in His example of obedience in the face of suffering.

Whether you have died to your desires or not, you will eventually find yourself in a position where you will have to choose between comfort, advantage, security, self-esteem, or pleasure, and the will of God.

God purposely steers us to these places where we must choose between our desire and His will. It is called His testing. In Psalms 11:5 we find, "The LORD tests the righteous." And again in Psalms 17:3, "You have tested my heart.... You have tried me and have found nothing; I have purposed that my mouth shall not transgress." Paul affirms this with, "We speak, not as pleasing men, but God who tests our hearts" (1 Thessalonians 2:4).

Abraham waited twenty-five years for his son of promise. This in itself was a test. Most people will not wait more than a few months for the promise of God. After Isaac was born, God waited until Abraham and he were very close before He gave Abraham another test.

Genesis 22:1, 2 And it came to pass after these things, that God did tempt Abraham, and said unto him, Abraham: and he said, Behold, *here* I *am*. And he said, Take now thy son, thine only *son* Isaac, whom thou lovest, and get thee into the land of Moriah; and offer him there for a burnt offering upon one of the mountains which I will tell thee of.

Notice the scripture specifically says, "God tested Abraham." Isaac was more dear than life to Abraham. Yet Abraham proved his love for God by offering his most precious possession. Abraham rose early in the morning and made the three-day journey to the place God showed him. He bound his son on the altar and raised the knife in obedience to God. Then the angel of the Lord said:

Genesis 22:12 And he said, Lay not thine hand upon the lad, neither do thou any thing unto him: for now I know that thou fearest God, seeing thou hast not withheld thy son, thine only *son* from me.

Let's look again at Abraham's great-grandson Joseph. God gave him a dream of leadership. God knew beforehand exactly how it would come to pass—Joseph's older brothers would turn on him and sell him into slavery. The Lord did not panic when his jealous brothers did this wicked thing. He knows the end from the beginning (Isa. 46:10). God did not author their evil behavior, but He did use the opportunity it afforded to test Joseph's heart.

Psalms 105:17-19 He sent a man before them, *even* Joseph, *who* was sold for a servant: Whose feet they hurt with fetters: he was laid in iron: Until the time that his word came: the word of the LORD tried him.

Joseph did not disobey or dishonor God. He believed in the dream, but even more he believed in the God who had promised it. God's promise was so real that Joseph clung to it in the midst of unbelief and adversity. He believed yet suffered. His obedience was accompanied by suffering. He faced the same temptation his descendants would later face in the wilderness. Would he complain, be offended and bitter toward God and his brothers, or would he learn obedience by that which he suffered? He chose obedience and endured suffering because he knew God was faithful. In the end he was greatly rewarded for faithfulness.

Joseph's descendants (the people of Israel) were also tested numerous times. But they had a different heart than what Joseph had. Over and over they failed and chose their own comfort, security, and pleasure over God's heart.

They were first tested when Pharaoh would not let them go, even after he'd seen the miracles. Because of the hardness of Pharaoh's heart, things got much worse for them. They were no longer supplied with straw for their quota of bricks. This meant that after a long day of toiling under the hot Egyptian sun they had to glean in the fields by night. In the face of this hardship, they complained to Moses (Exodus 5:6–21).

Later, after even mightier signs and wonders, Moses encouraged the people to believe God's promise of deliverance. But "they did not heed Moses, because of anguish of spirit and cruel bondage" (Exodus 6:9). It seemed the more God's plan was revealed, the worse it was for the descendants of Abraham. They were so discouraged they wanted to forget their dream of freedom and embrace Egyptian slavery. The pressure of their circumstances caused them to be mindful of the things of men rather than the plan of God.

When they left Egypt, God led them right up to the Red Sea where He once again hardened Pharaoh's heart so that Pharaoh pursued them. Now there was a sea before them and behind them a massive army waiting to butcher them. Watch the response of the Israelites.

Then they said to Moses, "Because there were no graves in Egypt, have you taken us away to die in the wilderness? Why

Exodus 14:11, 12 And they said unto Moses, Because *there were* no graves in Egypt, hast thou taken us away to die in the wilderness? wherefore hast thou dealt thus with us, to carry us forth out of Egypt? *Is* not this the word that we did tell thee in Egypt, saying, Let us alone, that we may serve the Egyptians? For *it had been* better for us to serve the Egyptians, than that we should die in the wilderness.

Notice the words, "it would have been better for us." This is a key statement; it revealed their disobedient hearts. They were more concerned about themselves than the will of God. This is exactly what Jesus was saying to Peter when He said, "You are not mindful of the things of God, but the things of men" (Matt. 16:23). The only way we can fulfill the will of God is to lay down our lives and trust in His loving care for us.

If not, we will abort His will whenever we perceive the suffering as more difficult than we can bear.

Even though they complained, God delivered Abraham's descendants by parting the Red Sea. They crossed over on dry ground and turned to watch those who had oppressed them for four centuries buried under the waters.

After seeing all this, Israel sang and danced with great joy. Oh the love and confidence they had for God now that they had seen Him move so mightily on their behalf. They would never doubt Him again! Right? Wrong!

Three days later God presented them with a new test.

Exodus 15:22-24 So Moses brought Israel from the Red sea, and they went out into the wilderness of Shur; and they went three days in the wilderness, and found no water. And when they came to Marah, they could not drink of the waters of Marah, for they *were* bitter: therefore the name of it was called Marah. And the people murmured against Moses, saying, What shall we drink?

Complaining is a form of rebellion. It murmurs that God's way is not the right way, His provision not good enough. Just three days after they saw God's mighty power they failed another test.

God provided the water they needed.

A few days later the people complained again because they were short of food. Disgruntled they murmured about how much better their food had been back in Egyptian slavery.

God told Moses, "Behold, I will rain bread from heaven for you. And the people shall go out and gather a certain quota every day, that I may test them" (Exodus 16:4).

This pattern of testing and rebellion repeated itself many times. Their constant rebellion caused them to never leave their place of testing. Hebrews sums up the sad story.

Hebrews 3:7-10 Wherefore (as the Holy Ghost saith, To day if ye will hear his voice, Harden not your hearts, as in the provocation, in the day of temptation in the wilderness: When your fathers tempted me, proved me, and saw my works forty years. Wherefore I was grieved with that generation, and said, They do alway err in *their* heart; and they have not known my ways.

"Their hearts were always looking somewhere else." This is the behavior of an individual who has elevated comfort over obedience. They will follow God into the easy places only to turn aside as the path becomes difficult. *Surely this is not God,* they assure themselves as the road takes a turn toward hardship. Their hearts may know this is the road God has for them, but they allow their minds to talk them out of it, asserting, "God wants me happy, at peace, and prosperous."

Hear what Paul has to say to the young churches in Lystra, Iconium and Antioch. He had returned to them to strengthen the souls of these new disciples. How did he accomplish this? He exhorted them with, "We must through many tribulations enter the kingdom of God" (Acts 14:22). Those who love "the good life" would question his statement, asking in disbelief, "Is that supposed to strengthen me?"

Hear what the Holy Spirit spoke through Paul to the Thessalonian believers.

2 Thessalonians 1:4, 5 So that we ourselves glory in you in the churches of God for your patience and faith in all your persecutions and tribulations that ye endure: *Which is* a manifest token of the righteous judgment of God, that ye may be counted worthy of the kingdom of God, for which ye also suffer:

This body of believers is commended by Paul. Today would we consider the hardships a sign of weak faith? Notice the statement, "He is using your sufferings to make you ready for His kingdom." Just as Jesus did, we learn obedience by what we suffer. This prepares us for His kingdom because spiritual growth progresses as we obey in the midst of suffering. This lends understanding to Paul's letter to the Philippian believers.

Philippians 1:29 For unto you it is given in the behalf of Christ, not only to believe on him, but also to suffer for his sake;

I was a believer for years before I recognized this scripture. I had passed over it many times because I did not believe in suffering. It did not fit my doctrine, so I omitted it. In my eyes all who suffered were either in sin or had not developed their faith. How immature!

When God opened my eyes to this truth, I had to laugh. Paul presents suffering as if it were a great honor or promise. "For to you it has been granted." You wonder, *What wonderful blessing has been granted to me?* Excited, you continue to read but then discover, "to suffer for His sake." What does Paul mean by "granted"? Is that a promise? Sounds more like a discouraging report!

But in fact, it is a promise because we are "heirs of God and joint heirs with Christ, if indeed we suffer with Him, that we may also be glorified together" (Romans 8:17). Those who suffer with Him will be glorified with Him. How do we suffer with Him? Paul amplifies this in his letter to the Colossians.

Colossians 1:24 Who now rejoice in my sufferings for you, and fill up that which is behind of the afflictions of Christ in my flesh for his body's sake, which is the church:

Paul had a strong understanding of suffering in his life because of the way the Lord called him into ministry. Paul received his calling from God through a man, Ananias, who prayed for him to receive his sight after his experience on the road to Damascus. Ananias was told, "Go, for he is a chosen vessel of Mine... For I will show him how many things he must suffer for My name's sake" (Acts 9:15–16). God prepared Paul for suffering from the very onset of his ministry. The Holy Spirit does the same for us by His Word.

1 Peter 2:21 For even hereunto were ye called: because Christ also suffered for us, leaving us an example, that ye should follow his steps:

You can understand Paul's final heart cry: "That I may know Him and the power of His resurrection, and the fellowship of His sufferings, being conformed to His death" (Philippians 3:10). The word *fellowship* means "participation with." Paul longed to participate with Christ in His sufferings, for he came to understand that in Christ's sufferings he found intimacy with Jesus.

In his earlier years Paul asked God to remove one of the hardships he was experiencing. He had yet to understand the purpose godly suffering played (2 Corinthians 12:7–9). Later he understood its purpose. Then Paul no longer requested a life free of suffering. "So for the sake of Christ, I am well pleased and take pleasure in infirmities, insults, hardships, persecutions, perplexities and distresses; for when I am weak (in human strength), then am I (truly) strong (able, powerful in divine strength)" (2 Corinthians 12:10, AMP).

Notice he said, "I am well pleased and take pleasure." Did he really say that? Yes, he had been caught up beyond the interest of self and had glimpsed the glory beyond hardship. That is why he could say to the Romans, "For I consider that the sufferings of this present time are not worthy to be compared with the glory which shall be revealed in us" (Rom. 8:18). Who is this us he referred to? All who have suffered as Christ.

Hear this wonderful promise:

1 Peter 4:12, 13 Beloved, think it not strange concerning the fiery trial which is to try you, as though some strange thing happened unto you: But rejoice, inasmuch as ye are partakers of Christ's sufferings; that, when his glory shall be revealed, ye may be glad also with exceeding joy.

If you look closely at these verses, you see that the greater the trial, the more you should proportionately rejoice. You will also notice that the extent to which you suffer with Christ's sufferings is the extent to which His glory will be revealed. This explains why the disciples rejoiced in their trials: they looked beyond the hardship into the realm of glory.

Those who rejoice in the furnace come out of the furnace. Those who murmur in the wilderness die in the wilderness. The children of Israel could not see beyond the desert. Joshua and Caleb saw past the suffering of the desert into the Promised Land of milk and honey.

Settle it in your heart that there will be hardships in serving the Lord. We do not need to look for opportunities to suffer. But as we live obedient to God they will present themselves. We are forewarned in this:

Many are the afflictions of the righteous.

—Psalms 34:19

Yet there is no defeat in the suffering of Christ! For the psalmist continued:

But the LORD delivers him out of them all.

—Psalms 34:19

Paul affirmed this:

But thanks be to God, who gives us the victory through our Lord Jesus Christ.

—1 Corinthians 15:57

Often our flesh will not be pampered as we obey God.

Jesus made it clear that to follow Him, there must be a denying of self by taking up the cross of death to self.

Therefore, since Christ suffered for us in the flesh, arm yourselves also with the same mind, for he who has suffered in the flesh has ceased from sin.

—1 Peter 4:1

A Christian who is not prepared to suffer is comparable to a soldier who goes to war unarmed! Can you imagine the United States sending our men to war without training and weapons? They would fail! Unarmed soldiers are either killed, captured, or severely wounded, unless they desert the battle and their duty, thereby accomplishing nothing. That's why Peter said, "Arm yourself."

Christians who are not armed to suffer respond to trials, afflictions, and persecutions with shock, bewilderment, or amazement. In this state of stupor they will react to the situation at hand as opposed to following the lead of their Commander.

Let me give you an example of one who is armed. A crucial part of training for airline pilots comes through the use of flight simulators. In these simulators pilots are confronted by almost every flight emergency they might face. In the safety of this setting they hone their response skills until they successfully face each situation. This arms them for emergencies. When something happens on an actual flight, they do not panic. They respond calmly, assisted by their extensive training. Even though the passengers may panic and give way to shock and hysteria, the pilot remains calm and in full control. Investigators who review black box tape recordings from crashes are amazed by the calmness of pilots. There is no panic in their voices even up to the moment of the crash. They are armed!

Jesus rebuked Peter for being mindful of the things of men. At that time Peter was not armed to suffer. Jesus was. This is confirmed by Luke 9:51, "Now it came to pass, when the time had come for Him to be received up, that He steadfastly set His face to go to Jerusalem." He would not be distracted from His course of obedience. He was unshakable in His resolve.

His twelve followers had quite a different perspective. Undoubtedly they were not armed to suffer.

Mark 10:32 And they were in the way going up to Jerusalem; and Jesus went before them: and they were amazed; and as they followed, they were afraid. And he took again the twelve, and began to tell them what things should happen unto him,

They were amazed! In shock! Their thoughts ran wild with fear: *How can He head toward Jerusalem, knowing what awaits Him there? I can understand that He knows He is destined to die, but I can't comprehend embracing it. Maybe it is just a possibility and will not happen.* Their thoughts were interrupted as Jesus pulled them aside to remind them He was going to Jerusalem to die. They were amazed and confused. Again their thoughts mocked them, *I don't understand. What good could this do anyone?*

Jesus was steadfast in His obedience; the disciples wavered in shock and uncertainty. Our maturity level is revealed in difficult times. How we handle persecution, tribulation, and other forms of hardship is a gauge for our true level of spirituality.

Jesus fulfilled His Father's will, yet not without a battle. The night before His crucifixion, He had to resist the temptation to preserve Himself. Under the pressure of this war He shed drops of blood (Matthew 26:36–44; Luke 22:44; Hebrews 12:3–4). We are told, "He humbled Himself and became obedient to the point of death, even the death of the cross" (Philippians 2:8). He humbled Himself and therefore was given grace from His Father to endure the suffering required by obedience. He endured the most awful and gruesome death known to mankind.

If we are to follow Jesus' example (1 Peter 2), we must arm ourselves in the same manner. Paul did so. He shared his armor with his disciples, the elders of Ephesus.

Acts 20:22, 23 And now, behold, I go bound in the spirit unto Jerusalem, not knowing the things that shall befall me there: Save that the Holy Ghost witnesseth in every city, saying that bonds and afflictions abide me.

How would we respond to prophetic words of persecution, hardship, and tribulation awaiting us at each turn? I am not implying that every genuine word from God should be of this nature, but there needs to be a balance.

A lot of our preaching and prophetic words have encouraged the wrong attitude in many believers. Our messages have been nice, comfortable, happy, or exciting. Our prophecies foretell prosperity and peace, all will be well. This encourages people to seek God for what He can do for them. The foundation of their love for Him shifts from who He is to what He can provide. They seek to fulfill the prophecy rather than obey the God of the prophecy. They are not interested in magnifying Jesus, whether by life or death (Philippains 1:20). They want their promise! They are not armed to suffer.

Many people surrounding Paul urged him not to go to Jerusalem because that was where it was prophesied he would suffer. However, Paul knew that Jerusalem was his directive from God. He declared that he would go no matter what happened.

Acts 20:24 But none of these things move me, neither count I my life dear unto myself, so that I might finish my course with joy, and the ministry, which I have received of the Lord Jesus, to testify the gospel of the grace of God.

Notice he was armed to suffer, and this gave him the ability to finish his race with joy. Many never start or complete their race because they are not prepared or because the way appears too difficult. It is like trying to run a marathon without ever training.

Some will be saved, but they will pass through fire first (1 Corithians 3:15). They had chosen to believe the wrong messages. They wanted preaching that would encourage them in their comfort. Tears shed at the judgment seat of Christ are extremely painful; they are shed in the light of the knowledge of what could have been if the course of obedience had been completed.

There are those who will finish their race with great joy. These are the overcomers—overcoming by the blood of the Lamb and the word of their testimony. They will not love their lives unto the death (Revelations 12:11).

Overcome! Let this be your aim, your goal and your testimony.

2

*

Humility the Road to Success

It seems that one of the hardest things to accomplish after a little ministry success is humility. A proud person blames everyone while excusing himself.

A person is the most susceptible to falling when he is doing well. When he reaches a level of success, it is easy to forget the grace that transported him there. Because this is true, we are to "be clothed with humility, for God resists the proud, but gives grace to the humble" (1 Peter 5:5).

Uzziah, a descendant of King David, was crowned king at the age of sixteen. At first he sought God diligently. You would too if you were made ruler of a nation at age sixteen. More than likely he was overwhelmed and humbled by the magnitude of the undertaking. Yet "as long as he sought the LORD, God made him prosper" (2 Chronicles 26:5). Because he utterly relied on God, he was greatly blessed. He made war against the Philistines, defeating them in numerous cities, as well as the Arabians, Meunites, and Ammonites. Under his lead the nation become strong both economically and militarily. There was an abundance of prosperity under his leadership.

All this success was the result of the grace of God on his life. But over time something changed: his humility was replaced by his own confidence.

2 Chronicles 26:16 But when he was strong, his heart was lifted up to

his destruction: for he transgressed against the LORD his God, and went into the temple of the LORD to burn incense upon the altar of incense.

It was not in a weak moment, but when Uzziah was strong, that his heart was lifted in pride. As he surveyed the prosperity and success that encompassed all his domain his heart ceased to seek the Lord. He could do it on his own now; he knew how. As his achievements mounted, he assumed God would continue to bless all he undertook just as God had done when he humbly sought Him.

His rise to pride did not happen overnight. But it can easily happen to anyone. God warned me, "John, most people in the kingdom who have fallen have not done so in the dry times, but in the times of abundance."

This is a pattern many Christians fall into. When they are first saved, they hunger to know the Lord and His ways. Their humility is evident because they seek Him and trust Him for everything. They arrive at church with a hunger in their hearts, "Lord, I want to know You!" They submit to God's direct and delegated authority. But after they have amassed knowledge and waxed strong through experience, their attitudes change.

Now, instead of reading their Bible with the intent of, "Lord, reveal Yourself and Your ways to me," they use it to support their established doctrine, reading what they believe instead of believing what they read. No longer do they listen for God's heavenly voice in the voice of their pastor. Instead they fold their arms and lean back with the attitude, "I'll see what he knows." They are experts in Scriptures but have forfeited their tenderness and humility of heart. The grace to serve God now wanes.

1 Corinthians 8:1 says, "We know that we all have knowledge. Knowledge puffs up [pride], but love edifies." Love does not seek its own but lays its life down for the Master and those it is called to serve. Pride seeks its own behind a mask of religion. God explained that knowledge gained without love results in pride.

When pride entered the heart of King Uzziah, did he become more or less religious? The amazing answer: he became more religious! His heart was lifted up, and he entered the temple to perform his so-called worship. Pride and a religious spirit go hand in hand. A religious spirit causes a person to think he is humble because of his appearance of spirituality. The truth is, he is proud. A proud person stays in bondage to a religious spirit because he is too proud to admit he has such a spirit! This is one reason pride is so well-camouflaged in the church. It hides behind a religious, charismatic, Pentecostal, or evangelical mask.

Azariah and the other eighty priests of the temple went into the sanctuary where Uzziah was burning incense and confronted him, saying, "It is not for you, Uzziah, to burn incense to the LORD... Get out of the sanctuary for you have trespassed! You shall have no honor from the LORD God (2 Chronicles 26:18). Watch Uzziah's response when confronted by the priests.

2 Chronicles 26:19 Then Uzziah was wroth, and *had* a censer in his hand to burn incense: and while he was wroth with the priests, the leprosy even rose up in his forehead before the priests in the house of the LORD, from beside the incense altar.

Uzziah became angry. Pride will always justify itself. This self-defense will be coupled with anger. A proud person blames everyone else while excusing himself. Uzziah directed his anger at the priests, but the problem lay deep within his own bosom. Pride had blinded his eyes! Instead of humbling himself, he allowed anger to fuel his pride. Leprosy broke out on his forehead where all could see it. In this case, leprosy was an outward manifestation of an inward condition.

Leprosy in the Old Testament is a type of sin in the New Testament. It is a sad but true commentary that many mighty people have fallen into sin in the church. One example is sexual sin. God spoke to me, "Bill, with many of these who fall into sin, the root is not the sin itself, but the root is pride."

Pride is a subtle and deadly foe yet so easily camouflaged. Those in pride are ignorant of their true condition. Only humility can expose it. Pride is the very root of rebellion, and we see its influence right from the start—when Lucifer rebelled against God. God described Lucifer's heart condition.

Ezekiel 28:14-17 Thou *art* the anointed cherub that covereth; and I have set thee *so:* thou wast upon the holy mountain of God; thou hast walked up and down in the midst of the stones of fire. Thou *wast* perfect in thy ways from the day that thou wast created, till iniquity was found in thee. By the multitude of thy merchandise they have filled the midst of thee with violence, and thou hast sinned: therefore I will cast thee as profane out of the mountain of God: and I will destroy thee, O covering cherub, from the midst of the stones of fire. Thine heart was lifted up because of thy beauty, thou hast corrupted thy wisdom by reason of thy brightness: I will cast thee to the ground, I will lay thee before kings, that they may behold thee.

All that he was and all that he possessed were a gift from God. Yet at some point he forgot this and longed for more. His heart became lifted up, and he wished to enforce his will. Issuing forth from the pride in his heart he made several proclamations, all which begin with the words, "I will" (Isaiah 14:12–15). There was no humility within him. He was cast out of God's presence.

Hear this, servant of the Lord. God gives grace to the humble while resisting the proud. You never find the grace of God in an individual who has forgotten where he came from and the One who brought him out. James said:

James 4:6, 7 But he giveth more grace. Wherefore he saith, God resisteth the proud, but giveth grace unto the humble. Submit yourselves therefore to God. Resist the devil, and he will flee from you.

We resist the devil by our submission to God. Our humility and obedience usher in God's grace, which is a mighty weapon against the evil one.

Hebrews 4:15, 16 For we have not an high priest which cannot be touched with the feeling of our infirmities; but was in all points tempted like as *we are, yet* without sin. Let us therefore come boldly unto the throne of grace, that we may obtain mercy, and find grace to help in time of need.

He gives us mercy and grace in order to help us. He is merciful toward our ignorance and weakness (1 Timothy 1:13; Hebrews 5:2) but not toward willful disobedience (Hebrews 10:26–31). He supplies the grace necessary to overcome our weakness.

In this light we have a new understanding of the truth: "My grace is sufficient for you, for My strength is made perfect in weakness" (2 Corinthians 12:9). Our weakness is our inability to obey God in our own strength. It is not possible to live the life God expects of us on our own. But He adds His strength to our weakness. This aid is called grace. So we can say grace gives us the ability to fulfill what truth demands. This is confirmed by Hebrews 12:28, "Therefore, since we are receiving a kingdom which cannot be shaken, let us have grace, by which we may serve God acceptably."

Receiving God's grace is not a onetime experience. James told believers, "But He gives us more and more grace" (James 4:6, AMP). We need it every moment of every day. In each epistle Paul begins with greetings of, "Grace to you from God our Father and the Lord Jesus Christ." These letters were for believers, illustrating our continual need for God's grace.

We are also encouraged to grow in the grace of God (2 Peters 3:17–18). As we do our hearts are strengthened to fulfill God's will and shun the will of man. We see this exemplified in the life of Jesus: "And the Child grew and became strong in spirit, filled with wisdom; and the grace of God was upon Him" (Luke 2:40). The grace of God on His life empowered Him to develop a strong spirit and fulfill the will of His Father.

There are various degrees of grace. This is revealed in Acts 4:33, "And with great power the apostles gave witness to the resurrection of the Lord Jesus. And great grace was upon them all." We should hunger for greater degrees of God's grace. The greater the grace, the greater our capacity to serve and glorify the Lord. And remember, God's Word says the pathway to grace is humility.

We are to walk continually in humility, for God gives His grace only to those who are of a contrite spirit (James 4:6–7), those who are utterly dependent upon Him. We see this humility or complete dependence upon God's grace in Paul.

2 Corinthians 12:9, 10 And he said unto me, My grace is sufficient

for thee: for my strength is made perfect in weakness. Most gladly therefore will I rather glory in my infirmities, that the power of Christ may rest upon me. Therefore I take pleasure in infirmities, in reproaches, in necessities, in persecutions, in distresses for Christ's sake: for when I am weak, then am I strong.

Hear his words, "The less I have, the more I depend on him." This was the progression of Paul's life. As you study it, you will find that the longer he lived, the more dependent on God's grace he became and the less he relied on his own strength. This attitude breeds humility. The longer Paul lived, the more he emptied himself for the sake of Christ.

When he was first saved, Paul humbled himself by forsaking all he had achieved in the flesh, laying aside all his accomplishments as nothing but vanity.

Philippians 3:7 But what things were gain to me, those I counted loss for Christ.

All who come to Jesus and are genuinely born again reach this place. However, humility does not stop there; it is progressive.

Proceeding with Paul as an example, he was a leader with an abundance of spiritual revelation and wisdom. This afforded him the opportunity to achieve much in his service to the Lord. But his knowledge easily could have become a stumbling block. He willingly released all he had achieved before his conversion, but what about after he became a Christian leader? Would he allow wisdom and accomplishment to lift his heart, or would he continue to depend upon God's grace? We find the answer in Paul's own words written after years of successful ministry.

1 Corinthians 15:9 For I am the least of the apostles, that am not meet to be called an apostle, because I persecuted the church of God.

Do you hear the humility in these words? He did not even consider himself worthy to be called an apostle because of the terrible things he did prior to his conversion. Yet this man received possibly the greatest revelation truth of God's forgiveness—that a man in Christ Jesus is a new creation. Previous moral and spiritual conditions have passed away, and all things have become new (2 Corinthians 5:17). Even with this revelation and the accompanying ministry exploits, he still remembered the magnitude and greatness of God's mercy toward him.

1 Corinthians 15:10 But by the grace of God I am what I am: and his grace which *was bestowed* upon me was not in vain; but I laboured more abundantly than they all: yet not I, but the grace of God which was with me.

"I labored more abundantly than all the other apostles"! Is Paul talking out of both sides of his mouth? This comment sounds arrogant, yet it is not. It precedes another declaration of Paul's dependence on God. He followed his assessment of himself as the least of the apostles with an acknowledgment that all he had done had only been by God's ability. He was fully aware that all he had achieved spiritually flowed from the unmerited favor and grace of God.

Paul wrote this letter to the Corinthians in A.D. 55. His self-description as "the least of all the apostles" is hard to swallow. Both in his day and throughout the history of the church, Paul has been esteemed as one of the greatest apostles. Now consider what he said to the Ephesians seven years later in A.D. 62 after further ministry accomplishments.

Ephesians 3:7, 8 Whereof I was made a minister, according to the gift of the grace of God given unto me by the effectual working of his power. Unto me, who am less than the least of all saints, is this grace given, that I should preach among the Gentiles the unsearchable riches of Christ;

Seven years earlier he called himself the least apostle, and now he describes himself as lower than the least of all the saints! What? If anyone could boast in their Christianity, it surely was Paul. Yet the longer he served the Lord, the smaller he saw himself. His humility was progressive. Could this be why the grace of God on his life increased proportionately the older he became?

At the close of his life Paul sent two letters to Timothy. Hear again how Paul described himself:

1 Timothy 1:15 This *is* a faithful saying, and worthy of all acceptation, that Christ Jesus came into the world to save sinners; of whom I am chief.

Now he is the "chief of sinners"! He did not say, "I *was* chief." He said,

"I *am* chief." After years of great accomplishment, his confession was not, "I have done it all; my great ministry should be esteemed." Nor did he say, "I have done a great work and deserve the respect of a true apostle." It was not, "I am the least of the apostles," as he had written several years earlier, nor was it, "I am least of the saints." It was, "Of all sinners, I am chief." Though he knew that in Christ he was the righteousness of God (2 Corinthians 5:21), he never lost sight of God's grace and mercy. In fact, the longer he lived, the more dependent he became on His grace.

This explains another statement Paul made toward the end of his life.

Philippians 3:13, 14 Brethren, I count not myself to have apprehended: but *this* one thing *I do,* forgetting those things which are behind, and reaching forth unto those things which are before, I press toward the mark for the prize of the high calling of God in Christ Jesus.

Can you hear the humility in his words: "I haven't arrived, and what I have achieved, I leave behind in thought. It is nothing compared to the quest to fully know Christ Jesus my Lord"?

Notice he said, "I press toward the goal." To press means there is resistance and opposition. One of the greatest opponents to the upward call is pride. That's the reason the upward call is so easy to miss.

We believers need to battle against the foe of pride rather than battle for our rights or privileges. We waste so much time defending ourselves. This leads to groups and contention.

Proverbs 13:10 Only by pride cometh contention: but with the well advised *is* wisdom.

By refusing to defend yourself, one if not both of the following will happen. First, you lay down pride, which will open your eyes to recognize flaws in your own character that went previously undetected. Second, if you are right, you are still following the example of Christ by allowing God His rightful place as judge of the situation.

1 Peter 2:19 For this *is* thankworthy, if a man for conscience toward God endure grief, suffering wrongfully.

1 Peter 2:21, 22 For even hereunto were ye called: because Christ also

suffered for us, leaving us an example, that ye should follow his steps: Who did no sin, neither was guile found in his mouth:

This is our calling: to follow Christ's example, who suffered when He was not at fault. This precept wars against the natural mind since its logic appears absurd.

However, the wisdom of God proves that humility and obedience make room for God's righteous judgment. Defense, correction, vindication, or whatever other response is appropriate should proceed from the hand of God, not from man. An individual who vindicates himself does not walk in humility of Christ. No one on earth possesses more authority than Jesus, yet He never defended himself.

Matthews 27:12-14 And when he was accused of the chief priests and elders, he answered nothing. Then said Pilate unto him, Hearest thou not how many things they witness against thee? And he answered him to never a word; insomuch that the governor marvelled greatly.

Jesus was accused of a complete lie! There was not a morsel of truth in what they accused Him of. Yet He did not correct his accusers or defend Himself. His behavior caused the governor to marvel at His composure. He had never seen such behavior from a man.

Why didn't Jesus defend Himself? It was so that He could remain under His Father's judgment and thus His protection. Remember Peter said, "When He was reviled, did not revile in return.... but committed Himself to Him who judges righteously" (1 Peter 2:23). When we refuse to defend ourselves we are hidden under the hand of God's grace and judgment. There is no safer place.

Romans 8:33 Who shall lay any thing to the charge of God's elect? *It is* God that justifieth.

In contrast, those who defend themselves come under the judgment of their accusers. The moment you justify or defend yourself before another you yield to them as your judge. You have forfeited your authority or position in Christ, for your accuser rises above you when you answer his criticism. Yes, his authority is elevated above you because of your self-defense. Attempting to prove your innocence, you succumb to the mercy of your accuser.

Matthews 5:25, 26 Agree with thine adversary quickly, whiles thou art in the way with him; lest at any time the adversary deliver thee to the judge, and the judge deliver thee to the officer, and thou be cast into prison. Verily I say unto thee, Thou shalt by no means come out thence, till thou hast paid the uttermost farthing.

According to this parable you will be made to pay whatever your accuser demands as restitution. You are left helpless and at his mercy. The greater the offense he bears toward you, the less mercy he will extend to you. He will exact every last penny of your debt.

Pride would say, "Defend yourself." Jesus said, "Agree with your adversary." In so doing you lay down pride and make God the judge of the situation.

3

ᵔᵕᵔ

The Fight of Faith

We all must learn to win in the fight of faith. This is a powerful Chapter that is sure to stir your fight. First of all disobedience is contagious.

Have you ever seen a person start their walk on fire for Jesus, only to end up in a lukewarm state after a process of time? You wonder, *How could someone so enthusiastic end up so weary in their walk?*

These people are the casualties of a battle they failed to recognize. Jude wrote a letter devoted entirely to addressing this conflict.

Jude 1:3 Beloved, when I gave all diligence to write unto you of the common salvation, it was needful for me to write unto you, and exhort *you* that ye should earnestly contend for the faith which was once delivered unto the saints.

Can you sense the urgency of the message? It is one of great importance. To contend is to battle or combat. The word *earnestly* indicates serious intent. We must ask this question, With what or with whom do we fight? I have heard different answers to this question. One suggests that we battle for the faith by speaking of our resistance toward demons in the Heavenlies. Though this is valid spiritual warfare (see Ephesians 6:10–12), it is not the fight of which Jude is speaking. We can find the answer in the next statement in his letter.

Jude 1:4 For there are certain men crept in unawares, who were before of old ordained to this condemnation, ungodly men, turning the grace of our God into lasciviousness, and denying the only Lord God, and our Lord Jesus Christ.

We must battle for the faith because certain individuals have slipped into our churches misrepresenting the grace of God as a cover-up or even license for sin.

The Greek word for *lewdness* is *aselgeia*. Strong's dictionary of Greek New Testament words defines this as "lasciviousness, unbridled lust or excess."

These individuals pervert the grace of God by living excessive, fleshly lifestyles while proclaiming their salvation by grace. The Living Bible sheds further light on this. It declares these people show "that after we become Christians we can do just as we like without fear of God's punishment" (Jude 4).

Jude said these men also "deny the only Lord God and our Lord Jesus Christ" (Jude 4). Some of you may be thinking, *No one could come into our churches today and speak out a denial of God and our Lord Jesus Christ.* You're right—anyone who tried to do that couldn't get away with it anymore today than they could in Jude's day. But Jude indicated these people *creep in unnoticed.* No one who openly denies Jesus as the Christ could remain unnoticed. The following verse sheds some light on how these people manage to creep in:

Titus 1:15, 16 Unto the pure all things *are* pure: but unto them that are defiled and unbelieving *is* nothing pure; but even their mind and conscience is defiled. They profess that they know God; but in works they deny *him*, being abominable, and disobedient, and unto every good work reprobate.

They do not deny the Lord by what they say but do so by their lifestyles or actions. At the same time they believe they know the Lord! Paul called such people impostors.

2 Timothy 3:13 But evil men and seducers shall wax worse and worse, deceiving, and being deceived.

An impostor is one who deceives others by an assumed character or false pretense (like the wolf in sheep's clothing). Paul did not limit their deception to others—he said their influence extended to their own selves. They really believe they serve the Lord. They confess a new birth experience, speaking fluently in the language of the Scriptures as they participate in Christian activities. The only way to discern them is by the fruit of their lives (Matthews 7:18–20).

These imposters "defile the flesh, reject authority, and speak evil of dignitaries" (Jude 8). They are "grumblers, complainers, walking according to their own lusts (desires); and they mouth great swelling words, flattering people to gain advantage. These are sensual [worldly minded] persons, who cause divisions" (Jude 16, 19). Is this not an accurate description of many who create problems in homes, ministries, and churches? Many naive, innocent people have been influenced by their behavior.

Jude 1:11 Woe unto them! for they have gone in the way of Cain, and ran greedily after the error of Balaam for reward, and perished in the gainsaying of Core.

He compares these people with three men of the Old Testament—Cain, Balaam, and Korah, all who at one time enjoyed fellowship with God or were in the service of God.

Cain presented a disobedient offering, became offended, rebelled against the counsel of God, and committed a murder.

Balaam was greedy for power, position, and money, and he prostituted the anointing on his life. Because of this, Balaam died by the edge of the sword at God's command (Joshua 13:22).

Korah was a priest and a descendant of Levi, yet he rose up in opposition to Moses and Aaron in the wilderness, claiming, "You take too much upon yourselves.... Why then do you exalt yourselves above the assembly of the Lord?" (Numbers 16:3). His concern was not that Moses was overburdened; he wanted a share of Moses' authority. His hidden agenda was to promote himself. Insubordinate to God's appointed leadership, he accused Moses (whom God had exalted) of exalting himself. By doing this, Korah set himself against God's authority (Romans 13:1–2). His rebellion was judged when he was swallowed alive by the earth (Numbers 16:31–33).

Cain, Balaam, and Korah were unable to maintain their relationships with God because their goal was to serve themselves. It was not the service of God or His people they sought. Jude described these people further by saying:

Jude 1:12 These are spots in your feasts of charity, when they feast with you, feeding themselves without fear: clouds *they are* without water, carried about of winds; trees whose fruit withereth, without fruit, twice dead, plucked up by the roots;

Love feasts were common meals eaten together by the early church. Any sort of Christian gathering today could represent a love feast. The imposters who attended these feasts were called "spots" because of their conduct. Jesus is coming back for a "glorious church, not having spot of wrinkle or any such thing" (Ephesians 5:27). Imposters will not be found in the assembly of the righteous on the Day of the Lord. Jude continues:

They are clouds without water, carried about by the winds.

—Jude 12

Clouds without water illustrate the emptiness of their condition. Though they bear a resemblance of godliness, they are void of the character of Jesus. They have the appearance of a believer without the life or substance of one. Take a careful look at the next statement made concerning these people.

Late autumn trees without fruit, twice dead, pulled up by the roots.

—Jude 12

Jude compares them to late autumn trees with no fruit. Autumn is the time of harvest when fruit should be fully ripe and hanging on the tree. He described these barren, uprooted trees as "twice dead." What a description—twice dead! In order to be twice dead you would have to be once dead, be made alive, and then die again. This describes people who were dead without Christ, then received salvation only to die again because they permanently departed from Him in their hearts.

A very deceptive doctrine has been propagated throughout the church. It claims that once an individual is saved there is no way they can ever lose their salvation. It is a controversial subject, yet it need not be. The only reason it is controversial is because some teachings have twisted the Scriptures until they say what we want to hear as opposed to God's truth. If a person's heart is set on an issue, they will funnel all Scripture through what they believe rather than believe what they read.

I challenge you to examine what the Bible has to say about it. Don't filter these scriptures through the teaching of Dr. So-and-So, but compare verse to verse and hear what the Spirit of God is saying. Listen with your heart; it will not lie to you. There is no reason to fear truth if you love God. For if you truly love Him, you will never want to leave Him!

We first need to determine which verses refer to individuals who have been saved. There is a good example in James.

James 5:19, 20 Brethren, if any of you do err from the truth, and one convert him; Let him know, that he which converteth the sinner from the error of his way shall save a soul from death, and shall hide a multitude of sins.

Notice James said "brethren" and "if anyone among you." He was not addressing those who just think they are Christians; he was describing a believer who had wandered from the way of truth. Again note that James called a brother who wandered from the truth a sinner. If they are not turned back by repentance, their destination is death. Jude described them as "twice dead." It is obvious from James these people were once alive in Jesus. The Book of Proverbs amplifies this point.

Proverbs 1:16 The man that wandereth out of the way of understanding shall remain in the congregation of the dead.

In order to wander from the truth you must first walk in it. But once a person wanders from the truth, if he or she does not return to the path of righteousness, their final destination will be "the assembly of the dead," which is hell. Peter wrote:

2 Peter 2:20 For if after they have escaped the pollutions of the world through the knowledge of the Lord and Saviour Jesus Christ, they are

again entangled therein, and overcome, the latter end is worse with them than the beginning.

Before we go on, ask yourself, would a person who has escaped the pollution of this world by the knowledge of the Lord Jesus Christ be saved? Without a doubt you should answer yes. So Peter is talking about people who have been saved. Now let's continue:

2 Peter 2:20b, 21 they are again entangled therein, and overcome, the latter end is worse with them than the beginning. For it had been better for them not to have known the way of righteousness, than, after they have known *it,* to turn from the holy commandment delivered unto them. These people returned to the world, were overcome by its power, and did not seek to restore their relationship to the Lord. Backsliders can return to the Lord through genuine repentance (we just read that in James).

But if they stay entangled it would have been better for them never to have known the way of righteousness. In other words, in God's eyes it is better never to have been saved than to receive the gift of eternal life and turn from it permanently.

How could it be better to have never known the way of righteousness? Jude answers this by saying they are "twice dead.... for whom is reserved the blackness of darkness forever" (Jude 12–13).

An eternity of blackest darkness is reserved for them. Those who received Jesus, knew His will, and still walked permanently away will receive the greatest punishment of the second death. (See Revelation 2:11; 20:6, 14; 21:8.) Jesus described their torment.

Luke 12:45-48 But and if that servant say in his heart, My lord delayeth his coming; and shall begin to beat the menservants and maidens, and to eat and drink, and to be drunken; The lord of that servant will come in a day when he looketh not for *him,* and at an hour when he is not aware, and will cut him in sunder, and will appoint him his portion with the unbelievers. And that servant, which knew his lord's will, and prepared not *himself,* neither did according to his will, shall be beaten with many *stripes.* But he that knew not, and did commit things worthy of stripes, shall be beaten with few *stripes.* For unto whomsoever much is given, of him shall be much required: and to whom men have committed much, of him they will ask the more.

A group of individuals who will expect to hear Jesus say enter into heaven but instead will hear Him say, "I never knew you; depart from Me you who practice lawlessness!" (Matthew 7:23). It is made up of people who join themselves to Jesus solely for the benefits of salvation. These people follow Jesus at first, but their lack of commitment is ultimately revealed (as in Judas Iscariot).

Now we meet the second group of people from Matthew 7:22– 23. These are those who lose their salvation, the ones who at one time knew Him and even did wonders in His name yet did not endure to the end. Jesus also rebuked these people with "I never knew you." How could this be?

Ezekiel 18:24 But when the righteous turneth away from his righteousness, and committeth iniquity, *and* doeth according to all the abominations that the wicked *man* doeth, shall he live? All his righteousness that he hath done shall not be mentioned: in his trespass that he hath trespassed, and in his sin that he hath sinned, in them shall he die.

God said He would not remember their righteousness. It would be as if it had never happened. This means He will forget it ever existed. It is as if He never knew this person. This is the reason Jesus will say to those who do not endure to the end, "I never knew you."

He will forget their righteousness just as surely as He will forgive and forget the sins of the righteous. He says, "This is the covenant that I will make with them after those days, saith the Lord, I will put my laws into their hearts, and in their minds will I write them; And their sins and iniquities will I remember no more" (Hebrews. 10:16–17, KJV).

God refuses to remember our sins. The devil will, and he accuses us. But God declares, "I have no remembrance of the sins you accuse them of!" In the eyes of God it is as though we have never sinned.

Let's summarize what Jude wanted to say. He urged us to fight earnestly for the faith and described the focus and nature of our battle.

The focus is upon those who say they are Christians but only obey God if it is convenient to their self-ruled life. Either they have never been believers, as in the case of Judas, or they have fallen from grace. Whichever the case, they are lukewarm impostors, false brethren, wolves in sheep's clothing, and spots in the church.

Virtually every voice of the New Testament—Jesus, Paul, Peter, Jude, and the apostle John—warned of those who would fall away. Likewise, I have joined my voice to their warning. Why? It is the voice of love spoken for the sake of protection! In this we discover the nature of our battle: to keep ourselves and those under our care from falling into the same state as these in disobedience.

After Jude warned of those who would pervert the grace of God, he gave us this strong exhortation of protection:

Jude 1:20, 21 But ye, beloved, building up yourselves on your most holy faith, praying in the Holy Ghost, Keep yourselves in the love of God, looking for the mercy of our Lord Jesus Christ unto eternal life.

We are to keep ourselves in the love of God. Remember, those who love God are obedient to Him (John 14:15). Jude warns of the leaven of disobedience filtering into your life. (See 1 Corinthians 5:6.) Disobedience is contagious. If you hang around a person with a contagious illness, your own resistance will eventually be worn down, and you will fall prey to it. It is the same with disobedience, but God's words of warning and instruction are like immunization shots. They boost our immunity and resistance to the virus of disobedience.

Suppose a very contagious disease was spreading throughout your community, but there was also an antidote to prevent the contraction of the disease. Would you immunize your children and teach them preventative health care? Yes, absolutely! We would afford them the protection of the antidote and educate them to prevent the spread of the disease.

Even so the Lord and those who penned His Word have gone to great lengths to warn us of the contagious diseases of luke-warmness and disobedience. Listen to the warning given to the elders of Asia:

Acts 20:28-31 Take heed therefore unto yourselves, and to all the flock, over the which the Holy Ghost hath made you overseers, to feed the church of God, which he hath purchased with his own blood. For I know this, that after my departing shall grievous wolves enter in among you, not sparing the flock. Also of your own selves shall men arise, speaking perverse things, to draw away disciples after them. Therefore watch, and remember, that by the space of three years I ceased not to warn every one night and day with tears.

Hear his words, "take heed." It is a warning he repeated night and day, pleading with tears for three years. He wanted to keep his spiritual children from the disease of disobedience. He said that wolves would come in among them. Jesus likened false prophets who come into the church to wolves dressed in sheep's clothing (Matthew 7:15). They talk like Christians but can be discerned by their fruit (Matthew 7:16). Wolves easily enter a flock when the shepherd is not protecting them.

Often we want to hear only encouraging and positive messages. However, Paul made it clear that to fully preach the gospel we must *warn* as well as *encourage*. By doing this we will present every man perfect in Christ Jesus (Colossians 1:28). Understanding and obeying the Bible's warnings from God are key elements in the completion of our journey in Christ.

David realized the value of God's precepts. He described them:

Psalms 19:9-11 The fear of the LORD *is* clean, enduring for ever: the judgments of the LORD *are* true *and* righteous altogether. More to be desired *are they* than gold, yea, than much fine gold: sweeter also than honey and the honeycomb. Moreover by them is thy servant warned: *and* in keeping of them *there is* great reward.

To the mature believer the entire counsel of God's Word is sweet, including His warnings. There is a great reward to those who take heed to them.

Ministers are called not only to feed God's sheep but also to protect them. They are to warn of the snares of the enemy. Many ministers have withdrawn from warning their people because they think it is a negative message. It is not negative but preventive—it saves lives and churches!

Jesus is certainly not negative, yet He said, "Take heed that no one deceives you" (Matthew 24:4). Again He charged His disciples, "Take heed, beware of the leaven of the Pharisees and the leaven of Herod" (Mark 8:15). The contagious leaven of the Pharisees was legalism, which leads to hypocrisy. The contagious leaven of Herod was a disobedient, fleshly lifestyle, which also leads to hypocrisy. These are two contagious diseases that can attack an unaware person and lead them into a disobedient lifestyle.

Peter warned us with, "You therefore, beloved, since you know this beforehand, beware lest you also fall from your own steadfastness, being led away with the error of the wicked" (2 Peter 3:17). Hear what he is saying. When a person is not warned, he can easily fall away from his steadfast obedience by the error of those who have already fallen.

Some of the most difficult places at which to minister are established Christian organizations. Christian schools seem to top the list. These institutions are hard to reach because they are lukewarm breeding grounds for rebellion and disobedience. It may start with a handful of students, often the most established. These young people have grown up in Sunday school and youth group and confess a born-again experience. Yet they are disrespectful to authority, bound by lust, and some have even experimented with drugs or alcohol at a young age. They are obsessed with professional sports figures, Hollywood, dating, and other worldly pursuits. Often they are the sons and daughters of the church leaders, yet they were not trained as children to discern compromise and hypocrisy. This makes them all the more callous and dangerous.

These hardened students seem unaware that their lifestyles preach a message to those around them. (What we live preaches louder than what we speak.) The message: you can be saved and still serve yourself and love the world.

This confuses the other students and new converts. Bewildered they ask, "How can Christians live like this?" At first they are shocked. Then reasoning sets in, and they conclude that God doesn't really care how they live. Rebellion is all right. The doctrine of perverted grace begins to permeate their thinking, encouraged by the lascivious lifestyle of their fellow students. There is more pressure to conform to the disobedience than to maintain a standard of godliness. Paul explained this dilemma.

1 Corinthians 5:6 Your glorying *is* not good. Know ye not that a little leaven leaveneth the whole lump?

I have learned that the prophetic anointing of God will arise stronger in the face of hardened people. The harder the people, the stronger the prophetic message. Yet it is for the sake of love and restoration, not for punishment. It often takes a good blow from a sledge hammer to crack a hardened heart. God says, "Is not My word.... like a hammer that breaks the rock in pieces?" (Jeremiah 23:29).

Jesus is not coming back for a lukewarm bride who fornicates with the world. He is coming for a consecrated bride, unspotted by the world. Would you marry someone who said, "I'll be faithful to you for 364 days a year, but give me one day a year to jump in bed with my old lovers"? Of course not! Neither would Jesus. He is not coming for a bride who has reserved a portion of her heart for the world! Don't be deceived. Don't be contaminated. Don't be infected by the subtlety of disobedience. Do not stray from your steadfast post to be led away to a lukewarm cesspool.

I challenge you to read the Bible in the light of what the Spirit of God has revealed to you through these last two chapters. I realize this message may not have lifted you to a new dimension of happiness, but it holds a wealth of understanding and wisdom that will guard your eternal joy at the possible expense of your temporary happiness. May the grace of our Lord be with you.

4

~

The World's Great Needs, Can They Be Met?

Leadership within the Church needs to realize there are big needs that need to be met.

Matthew 9:36 But when he saw the multitudes, he was moved with compassion on them, because they fainted, and were scattered abroad, as sheep having no shepherd.

I have stood before great crowds containing some of the most heartbreaking sights of human need imaginable, and I have met privately with very high-ranking leaders. Yet I can truthfully say I have never met a person who did not have some kind of need. You have never met a person who does not have needs, whether or not you are aware of them.

It is not enough, however, just to realize that people have needs. Neither is it enough to be moved with compassion for them. We must provide the answer and the help if we are to work the works of God in our generation. Is there an answer for them? What can you tell them? Where can they find real help?

God has greatly blessed us. One of the greatest things I have to offer is the strength of my prayers, not only in meetings, but alone with God in the power of intercession.

To provide answers is precisely the reason for the preparation of this

Chapter. It puts into your hands a manual on spiritual warfare. It reveals the basic force, power, and cause behind all human suffering and tells what you, as a child of God, a member of God's Army, can do about it. Victory is yours!

I pray that these truths will touch your life with the fire and power of God to meet the desperate needs of those in your area of influence.

2 Timothy 2:2 And the things that thou hast heard of me among many witnesses, the same commit thou to faithful men, who shall be able to teach others also.

5

~

Church Leaders at Greater Risk?

This whole book is for Church Leaders whether new to it or have been in leadership for years. You must first realize that leaders are at greater risk. Fear, suspicion, and mistrust exploded in the church. Friendships faded, confidences were broken. What I had falsely assumed to be solid personal relationships, on which I had depended on for years, began to disintegrate before my eyes. The pulpit became a place where the most intimate of secrets were publicly shared to bolster the pastor's position. Clearly, sides were being drawn.

A Dr. Jekyll to Mr. Hyde kind of metamorphosis started to affect the highest spiritual authority in the church — namely the pastor. Almost overnight his long-held fears and lifelong insecurities erupted into brutal retaliatory accusations, charges, and threats. He lashed out against members of the church with no regard for their personal well-being. His behavior reflected the heart of a King, not a true shepherd. A rampage of terror not unlike the original Dr. Jekyll and Mr. Hyde scenario took over this once beloved leader. A cleverly disguised but deadly assailant wreaked havoc on an unsuspecting church population, taking a number of lives in the process.

Soon, I would become a child of a spiritual divorce. The twist in this divorce was that the parents would divorce the child. Suddenly, tragically, I, too, would be forced to start over. Where would I find a new spiritual family? Where would I find another spiritual father and mother? Could I survive without them? Reluctantly, like an orphan, I had to begin my search for a new spiritual home and family. Sadly, my beloved home church, the church of those wonderful early years as a newborn Christian, was no longer a safe place.

Like an orphan, I battled with feelings of betrayal, abandonment, and loneliness. No one ever asks to be an orphan, and I was no exception; but an orphan I would become. I decided we had no other recourse but to leave. Within six months of our departure from the church, me — along with thirty other families — were publicly excommunicated. Were disagreement, diversity, and differences sin let alone grounds for excommunication? I didn't think so. But I soon learned the leadership of my former church did.

During this public, Sunday morning event, the curse-like decree to "note those who cause division.... and avoid them" (Romans 16:17) was publicly issued from the pulpit. Within this context, a deadly Christian curse, led by my former pastor, was eventually launched against me by my former church. On one hand, it was a miscarriage of justice and a misinterpretation of Scripture. On the other hand, it was the best thing that ever happened to me! Through this public excommunication, I would die that day to everything I had become.

A closer look at Romans 16:17-18 — the passage so often used against me — reveals some interesting points.

Romans 16:17, 18 Now I beseech you, brethren, mark them which cause divisions and offences contrary to the doctrine which ye have learned; and avoid them. For they that are such serve not our Lord Jesus Christ, but their own belly; and by good words and fair speeches deceive the hearts of the simple.

Paul was writing about Judaizers and their attempts to pervert the gospel of the Lord Jesus Christ. He was not talking about disagreements among Christians or about church members disagreeing with Christian leaders. In verse 17, Paul identifies these individuals as those who "cause divisions and offenses contrary to the doctrine which you have learned."

He was referring to the doctrine of orthodox New Testament Christianity and not to a difference of opinion among Christians. He was not licensing leaders to excommunicate other Christians because someone disagreed with them. He was not referring to a list of homemade, arbitrary rules and regulations that found their origin in a single man or church. Paul was defending the gospel of Jesus Christ — not himself!

Paul was not warning one church about those who may have disagreed with their pastor and decided to attend another church. Paul was warning Christians about *non*-Christians. These individuals whom Paul noted and avoided were "not serving the Lord Jesus Christ" and were causing others to forsake the teachings of Paul.

This convenient misuse of the Bible were characteristics of my original church's methods. Whenever it served them, they used the Bible for their own end. When the Bible did not support their practices, they easily misinterpreted it to suit themselves. Romans 16:17-18 is an example of this distorting of Scripture to their own destruction. The apostle Peter wrote that this tendency is a sign of instability and ignorance. Peter said that those who distort the proper interpretation and application of the Bible do so "to their own undoing, to their own ruin" (2 Peter 3:16).

Ironically, the only division in this whole tragic episode was caused by the leadership of the church. They publicly demanded that people with a dissenting viewpoint leave. To make matters worse, they received accusations against me from others without ever checking on the reliability of the information. Biblical "due process" was never followed.

The church leadership initially drew the battle lines by forcing people to choose sides. If there was a battle, they fired the first shot. I never wanted a fight, and I certainly never wanted a war. I knew how David must have felt when he wrote, "I am for peace: but when I speak, they are for war" (Psalms 120:7). If there was any division, clearly the church leaders created it. I always wanted as good a relationship as any two disagreeing parties could have. In my wildest imaginations, I never dreamed anything as vengeful and vindictive could come from fellow believers. Their retaliatory behavior caught me completely off guard. I had never expected to witness such dissension, prejudice, and bigotry among Christians. Jesus said that sometimes your enemies "would be those of your own household." He was right, and it hurt deeply.

The temptation for me to strike back in retaliation was tremendous. More than once my flesh wanted to get even. During this period, however, an important death took place that had a profound effect on my life. It was a death that took place inside of me — I was the host. All my attempts at self-justification had failed. My efforts to explain my rightness were futile. Everything I did in my flesh to rescue my good name, Christian reputation, and leadership profile backfired miserably. As important to God as these things are, they were the "Isaacs" that I needed to place on my altar of sacrifice. These were the things I held dearly that God required of me to sacrifice back to Him. All this had to die.

I had no permission then — and I have been given no permission at present — to allow even a hint of retaliation, retribution, or revenge on these pages. This is how God has worked His will in my life. It is how He has kept contamination off these pages. He killed everything in me that was not of Him. He did not vindicate me when I wanted Him to or the way I wanted Him to. God frustrated every attempt I made at trying to survive the assassination of my character, reputation, and ministry. The Lord wasted no time in crucifying everything in me, effectively destroying my kingdom and releasing His kingdom in me.

"I know, O Lord, that Your judgments are right, and that in faithfulness you have afflicted me" (Psalms 119:75). Infinitely more important to God — and immeasurably more beneficial to me — was the suffering, persecution, and the "valley of the shadow of death" God had prepared for me. It was years before I understood this and finally embraced it as the will of God. In other words, I was resisting what I should have been embracing!

Before, during, and after my public excommunication, the pastor never once attempted to discuss my so-called sin with me in person. In fact, this whole tragic episode took place without this pastor ever once talking to me! Along with others, I was publicly excommunicated by my former pastor, who had the support of his entire congregation. These former "brothers and sisters" never once raised any questions as to his actions. Such a lack of proper biblical protocol is hard to believe, but this is exactly how it happened.

As the years went on, numerous attempts were made on my part to discuss the issues. I made phone calls and left messages — all to no avail. I wrote letters and even involved two other pastors in an attempt to bring some closure to this ugly wound. Sadly, nothing has worked.

My former pastor never once approached me personally to bring healing to this terrible wound. He never once communicated to me what the issue or issues were that (in his mind) merited excommunication and public dis-fellowship. Excommunication is one of the most severe forms of church discipline one Christian could ever bring against another, yet no explanation occurred. He never told me what I had done and never revealed — even to this day — what my alleged gross sin was.

I had to assume the charges he levied against me were of a serious nature because of the penalty he demanded I pay. If the sentence always fits the crime, in his eyes I must have committed the spiritual crime of the century! To the pastor, this was about sin and punishment.

Sin is the worst charge you can bring against a Christian. To say someone has sinned is to condemn that person. It is the most severe form of judgment. If this judgment had been a righteous judgment (which it was not), based on the written Word of God (which it was not), with collaborating witnesses and ample evidence (which it was not), then the pastor would have been just in his judgment of me.

These charges were little more than one man's self-righteous personal vendetta. How do I know? Because of the facts: there was no sin worthy of excommunication; no biblical support for his actions; the absence of unbiased, impartial witnesses; and the nonexistence of even the most minute bit of evidence or proof.

My public excommunication was not an issue of church discipline nor about administering correction. The pastor was not concerned about restoring a fallen comrade in the "spirit of meekness" — as Galatians 6:1

suggests. How do I know? Because my spiritual welfare was never considered. This was about one man's insatiable appetite to be pre-eminent, pre-dominant, and premier. This entire episode was, in fact, an attempt by the Holy Spirit of God to expose a deeply entrenched narcissistic personality in the pastor. His excessive admiration of himself and his overtly self-important spirit were the real issues.

It was God who decided — long before I knew what He was doing — to use me as the catalyst to bring this exposure to the forefront. In my mind this attempt failed, but that is the Holy Spirit's concern. My place is to love those who mistreat me and pray that God's mercies would be extended to them. I continually reminded myself of Solomon's words:

Proverbs 24:17-20 Rejoice not when thine enemy falleth, and let not thine heart be glad when he stumbleth: Lest the LORD see *it,* and it displease him, and he turn away his wrath from him. Fret not thyself because of evil *men,* neither be thou envious at the wicked; For there shall be no reward to the evil *man;* the candle of the wicked shall be put out.

The pastor may have climbed to the top of the ministry ladder at the expense of far too many Christian lives. He became a sort of predator, destroying and devouring those he perceived as opponents. Whatever God had intended as a source of adjustment in this man's life was viewed as life-threatening. In fact, these God-ordained adjustments were meant to be life-saving. If only they had been seen as such and embraced.

The extremes that caused this mess in the first place were the very issues these adjustments could have remedied. The very areas of personal weakness that produced this ministry's erratic behavior could have been balanced through humility and submission to God's Word. The pastor's life and ministry would have vastly improved, and the kingdom of God would have benefited. His ministry could have been measured in numbers of spiritual children growing to full maturity instead of numbers of spiritual casualties.

Are Christian leaders — those who guard, feed, and guide the sheep — exempt from the temptation to curse just because they occupy a position of spiritual authority, trust, and influence in the church? Does their level of spiritual maturity guarantee that they will never participate in any curse or curse-like activity? Are these leaders somehow above cursing because they have obviously been promoted by God to positions of oversight, representing God's government in the church? I wish I could answer yes to these questions, but I cannot. In fact, the opposite may be true of leaders. They may face greater temptation to use cursing as a manipulative spiritual weapon.

We are told by God's Word to follow, obey, submit, honor, and support our spiritual leaders. We all should be grateful for our church leaders and thank God for them daily. Indeed, our spiritual leaders are gifts to the church. But they certainly are not above the temptation to curse — no matter how gifted! No one — lay person or leader — is ever immune from the potential to curse another. A leader may be successful in God, possessing a high level of gifting with an apparent anointing by God on his life. He may pastor a large thriving church. Yet, no matter how prominent a profile he may seem to have, any leader can yield to the temptation to curse.

In fact, Christian leaders may be especially vulnerable to temptation when discussing the potential to curse other Christians! I did not say they are necessarily more vicious or that they actually do more cursing than others, or that they do any cursing at all. I simply stated that a leader faces a greater *temptation* to curse. Why is this temptation to curse especially true among leaders? The explanation to this bold statement lies in understanding the very make up of a leader.

The same spiritual skills that make a person a leader can be either his greatest asset or his greatest liability depending on how he uses them. I call this "the Saul syndrome." The spiritual pendulum of intent can swing both ways, and a leader must choose daily exactly how he will be a "steward of the mysteries of God" (1 Corinthians 4:1). He has two decisions he must constantly make:

A leader must realize that how he does his job may not be as important as why he does his job.

A leader can perform his appointed function for the glory of God, or he can relegate his ministry to a self-promoted, self-serving, self-important showcase of his pseudo-spirituality and soulish charisma as King Saul did.

Like Saul, a leader can draw attention to himself or to the God who made him.

This is a hard choice; but a choice a leader must make daily. Why? Because so much of what a leader does is a matter of the heart. As long as Saul "remained small in his own eyes," there was no problem. The prophet Samuel even pointedly asked the king, "When you were little in your own eyes, were you not head of the tribes of Israel? And did not the Lord anoint you king over Israel?"

(1 Samual 15:17). The minute King Saul's heart was filled with pride, self-will, and self-love, it was not long until the kingdom was literally ripped from him. "Because you have rejected the word of the Lord, He also has rejected you from being king" (v. 23), Samuel prophesied. The example of King Saul teaches us two facts:

Leadership in God is a position of incredible responsibility.

Why? If for no other reason than God Himself has called that person to be a leader.

This leader called by God is caring for God's most prized possession.

And what is that? His sheep. His people!

Because of these two facts, God equips His leaders with supernatural tools to do the job He has called them to do. How a leader uses these tools is the point I am trying to make. By virtue of a leader's position, God has taught him how to direct God's power, release God's influence, bring about the change God desires, and literally revolutionize a person's life under that leader's spiritual care.

The potential always exists to abuse power — no matter what arena we are discussing — whether political, military, financial, or spiritual. As long as spiritual power can be abused, the potential for curses will exist; and as long as leaders are entrusted with this power, leaders will face a greater temptation to misuse their power in order to curse. King Saul fell into the power trap, and in the process shot himself in the foot.

During a victory dance, the Israelites sang and compared Saul's "thousands" to David's "ten thousands." From that day on, "Saul kept a jealous eye on David" (v. 9). As a faithful, loyal servant, David was simply doing his duty. He had no intention of trying to assume the king's position. Nevertheless, from that day forward Saul, possessed by an evil spirit, began to target David. At one point, the king tried to pin David against the wall with a spear!

This same "Saul spirit" dangerously motivates Christian leaders today through jealousy, anger, and pride — not to mention fear: "Saul was afraid of David" (v. 12). When these emotions create a perceived threat to the leader's own kingdom, he often responds with rejection, retaliation, and finally annihilation. In other words: Eliminate the competition! David must be killed.

Finally, Saul became the confirmed enemy of David, the exact opposite purpose God had intended. "So Saul became David's enemy continually" (v. 29). In fact, Saul's failure or refusal to acknowledge David's anointing from God sped up the king's own fall from grace and cost him the king-dom. Although David was an asset, Saul viewed him as a liability. Countless leaders today make the same mistake. I wonder how many leaders have rejected the "David's" God has sent them.

Sadly, my former pastor acted selfishly and vindictively out of a Saul spirit of personal vengeance. Driven by fear of losing the dominance and control over his flock, which he so desperately needed to fill the emotional cavity in his own person, he made me his enemy. What Jesus wanted to heal in him (like Saul), the pastor filled with performance, position, and personal power. His emotional emptiness and instability, coupled with an inability to grasp the love of God for himself, had been compensated by a lifelong history of doctrinal and practical extremism. Everything he believed (his doctrine) was formed and influenced by this extremist "spirit."

This absurd incident was not about defending God or Jesus, the Bible, the church, or a particular theology or creed. This calculated assault on me resulted from the pastor's personal paranoia. He thought I wanted to take over his church. He thought I wanted to be the pastor. How do I know this? How can I make this accusation? He told me so. Several years earlier, while I was still attending the church in question, he confronted me with his fears.

Being the senior pastor of that church, however, was the farthest thing from my mind. The threat I posed to him was imagined on his part. I loved him and supported him. I laid my life down for him. Like David, there was no more faithful servant or disciple than I. Even after giving him my all, he still wrestled with the fear that something would be taken from him. I was not the first he had accused and was not to be the last.

Suspecting, accusing, demeaning, and belittling others (both individuals and churches) became the spark that fired the engine of the pastor's justification. By putting down others, he falsely assumed he was elevating his own life and ministry.

It is a sad day when we have to live our lives in fear that what God has given us man can take away. Pride has a way of blinding us to the hideous nature of sin. Yet, sin is sin. Our faith slips from its foundation, and we find ourselves sinking in the stench of religious hypocrisy. What is the criteria for hypocrisy? Saying we love God while hating our brother.

He who says he is in the light, and hates his brother, is in darkness until now. He who hates his brother is in darkness and walks in darkness, and does not know where he is going, because the darkness has blinded his eyes. We know that we have passed from death to life, because we love the brethren. He who does not love his brother abides in death Whoever hates his brother is a murderer, and you know that no murderer has eternal life abiding in him. If someone says, "I love God," and hates his brother, he is a liar; for he who does not love his brother whom he has seen, how can he love God whom he has not seen?... He who loves God must love his brother also "(1 John 2:9-11; 3:14-15; 4:20-21).

When we destroy other lives without a hint of remorse or a single pang of guilt, we have crossed over a very serious line. No longer Christ-like, we become Christian butchers, carving up others and serving them on trays of hatred and egocentric pride. We lose — sometimes permanently — the love of God, becoming loveless, use-less, meaningless beings and not followers of Jesus Christ and His example. Cursing is a tool of spiritual tyranny — a weapon only a cowardly tyrant would use. A tyrant is one who rules with harshness, cruelty, and oppression

Are there spiritual tyrants in the church? As long as the potential to misuse power exists, tyrants will continue to abuse others — even in the church. When a Christian leader exercises spiritual power unjustly, selfishly, or cruelly, a curse risks being implemented by that Christian. If you or anyone you know has ever used spiritual skills, talents, or intentions in a decisively destructive manner, you or he risks becoming just such a spiritual tyrant. Take this test to see if you are at risk:

- Have you ever prayed against someone, especially another Christian?
- Have you ever punished people with your speech, through gossip and slander, or controlled or manipulated another through your prayers?

Have you ever used the Bible in a self-serving way, quoting Scripture against another in a destructive manner? Such actions do not necessarily mean you are not saved, but it does Christian cursing Christians mean you are greatly misled. Obviously, you need to repent!

What is the basis for this potential abuse by leaders? It is the same with all those who possess any measure of power or authority. The problem is basic human nature.

Selfishness.

As long as leaders harbor attitudes of self-seeking, bitter envy, jealousy, pride, competition, contention, rivalry, stubbornness, and unbridled ambition, there exists the opportunity for personal curses to form and be unleashed in the church by these same leaders.

Unbroken ego.

As long as church leaders possess unbroken egos and abusive understandings of spiritual authority, they risk becoming spiritual tyrants. The symptoms manifest them-selves in the need to retaliate and an addiction to spiritually control others. When this kind of behavior is present, there will be curses in the church. Since such temptations are faced more by leaders than ministry leaders, the potential to curse is increased among leaders. God has called leaders to a higher level of accountability, integrity, and honor.

Misuse of ministry.

When leaders break the trust given them by God through a misuse of their ministries, gifts, abilities, talents, and "anointings," they risk perverting their "call" and potentially misdirecting any spiritual skills they may possess. When this happens, a leader's ministry will achieve less than optimum results. At most, he can trespass into an area of spiritual activity that relies on demonic soul power and borders on Christian witchcraft — if not actual witchcraft! A leader may even end up like Samson who did not know that the Lord had left him until after it was too late! (See Judges 16:20.)

How does a leader misdirect his God-given spiritual skills? By what means can a leader renege on the standards imposed on him by God and direct these skills in a destructive direction? How does a leader become counter-productive to God's purpose for his life and a detriment to the kingdom of God — although genuinely called and gifted by God? Is this even possible? Can such a thing actually happen? As with most all leadership issues, the underlying symptoms for abuse seem to be a matter of the leader's heart. What are the warning signs that a leader may be a risk?

A lack of clear biblical objectivity becomes evident.

No matter how seemingly insignificant at first, this tendency can give birth to extremism, fanaticism, and heresy.

The Word of God is relegated to a subservient role.

Instead of preeminent, the Scriptures become subordinate to the whims, opinions, feelings, and judgments of a particular theological prejudice or dogma, and further tainted by the leader's inevitable fallibility.

The leader's opinions become deified in the minds of his followers.

His words are raised to near divine rank. Gradually, the leader's words become "God's" words whether or not the Bible agrees! This adoration of both doctrine and leader creates the same self-deception that is characteristic of all Christian cults. This is why cults equate leaving their group with leaving God. To those faithful to the cult, the cult is God and the leader the clear object of their worship!

God's warnings and disciplines are rejected.

When any church ignores the changes required of a loving God and circumvents His timely adjustments, they are asking for trouble. Either that church allows Jesus to prune them, thus producing better fruit, or He takes the next more severe step: He "lays the ax to the root" and starts over by planting a new tree.

A third possibility also exists. When the tree dies, sometimes those around it leave it standing and ornate it with artificial fruit. Some even begin to love the withered tree more than the fruit it is supposed to produce. Make no mistake about it, the tree is dead and the fruit is artificial.

A greater temptation to use cursing can exist among leaders. Why? Here are a few reasons:

Leaders have been called to a higher level of accountability.

If this higher level of accountability is denied, refused, or ignored, deception results. Their own disobedience exposes them to greater risk as far as keeping their individual anointing pure and uncontaminated.

Leaders have been entrusted with incredible spiritual power.

If this power is prostituted, greater spiritual abuse results. An abuse of supernatural power always precedes cursing.

Leaders possess a highly refined skill level, which they use to access this awesome spiritual power.

This skill is what makes them leaders in the first place. As leaders they can effectively release either the power of God and heaven — or the power of Satan and hell — depending on the condition of their own lives! A leader's misuse of spiritual skills, governed by a heart that has not been kept pure, always precedes cursing. How can a leader avoid falling into the curse trap? A true leader must:

- Always be honestly accountable to others — especially peers.

- Never abuse his ability or privilege to access supernatural power.
- Constantly guard the condition of his heart — his source of motivation.

Actually, this is good advice for any Christian who wants to avoid participating in curse-like activity.

If a leader thinks he cannot be replaced, he will go to any length to keep himself indispensable, even to the extreme of eliminating any and all dis-sent. Dictators, tyrants, and generals have done this for centuries, but it is not supposed to be this way among Christian brothers! The pastor of my former church had no real charges, no real evidence, and no real witnesses against me. Most alarming of all, he had no biblical support. All he had was his fear, insecurities, and a twisted sense of self-importance.

The spiritual atmosphere of long-term, unchallenged, spiritual absolutism in the church produced the inevitable results. Spiritual fatalities were strewn everywhere, attesting to the abuse of power vested in one man. Unfortunately, the old adage is true even in spiritual matters: "Power corrupts, and absolute power corrupts absolutely." To determine which power a Christian leader releases, answer the following three questions:

- What is the general condition of his own heart? Is he moldable, flexible, and pliable? Is he genuinely teachable?
- Has he responded to God's dealings in his life in a positive, humble manner; or is he obstinate, arrogant, proud, and unyielding to others — especially his peers?

? Does he personally operate under spiritual authority?

If a leader is inflexible, arrogant, and rebellious, he cannot help but direct curse-like power against others. Why? The sin-stained condition of his hardened heart, his refusal to submit to the correction and adjustments of his loving heavenly Father, and his independent spirit make cursing almost second nature.

I have a warning for the perceived enemies of a leader like this: Watch out! This type of leader will eventually unleash this evil power against you. He will curse you without blinking an eye and all the while think he is doing a truly righteous thing! Truly, a leader possessing these qualities is a dangerous man, both to others and to himself. And I dare say, such leaders are resident in the church. How do I know? Because I was the victim of a pastor's curse.

6

❧

God's Family

God has set things to be a certain way within the Church. God's plan for how the Body of Christ is to operate can be found in the early Church.

Acts 2:1-4 And when the day of Pentecost was fully come, they were all with one accord in one place. And suddenly there came a sound from heaven as of a rushing mighty wind, and it filled all the house where they were sitting. And there appeared unto them cloven tongues like as of fire, and it sat upon each of them. And they were all filled with the Holy Ghost, and began to speak with other tongues, as the Spirit gave them utterance.

They were in one place and in one accord. That means that they weren't too busy with their own selfish ambitions, but they were there to fulfill what Jesus had asked them to do before He ascended into Heaven. Jesus told them to stay there in the city until they were sent a "Comforter." Essentially, they were to stay until they received the Holy Spirit, which is what happened on the day of Pentecost.

The Church was to come together. They were to get out of their homes and come together in unity. We hear about people who want to flow in the Holy Spirit—they want the gifts and the signs and wonders—but they don't want to stay in unity. The Church needs to come together in unity if they want the blessing that God has for them.

Psalms 133:1-3 **A Song of degrees of David.** Behold, how good and how pleasant *it is* for brethren to dwell together in unity! *It is* like the precious ointment upon the head, that ran down upon the beard, *even* Aaron's beard: that went down to the skirts of his garments; As the dew of Hermon, *and as the dew* that descended upon the mountains of Zion: for there the LORD commanded the blessing, *even* life for evermore.

The oil being poured is the anointing.

Romans 15:5 Now the God of patience and consolation grant you to be likeminded one toward another according to Christ Jesus:

Colossians 3:13-15 Forbearing one another, and forgiving one another, if any man have a quarrel against any: even as Christ forgave you, so also *do* ye. And above all these things *put on* charity, which is the bond of perfectness. And let the peace of God rule in your hearts, to the which also ye are called in one body; and be ye thankful.

Ecclesiastics 4:12 And if one prevail against him, two shall withstand him; and a threefold cord is not quickly broken.

Deuteronomy 32:29-31 O that they were wise, *that* they understood this, *that* they would consider their latter end! How should one chase a thousand, and two put ten thousand to flight, except their Rock had sold them, and the LORD had shut them up? For their rock *is* not as our Rock, even our enemies themselves *being* judges.

When we are in unity, we are a force to be reckoned with against the darkness. That is why unity is so rare in churches and relationships. It's usually the first thing to get attacked. The devil knows, especially if you are a cutting-edge church, you are a force that is messing with the kingdom he is trying to establish. He knows he has no power against what you can do, so he whispers lies into the ears of the leaders. He whispers offenses over and over until you act on it. He attacks the Church from within. It's like a special forces mission. He sends his troops on the inside to break down the unity so that the work can be destroyed. But we don't have to listen to him. We can stop the forces of darkness coming into the Church. We can be in unity. We can work together as a team.

2 Corinthians 12:10 Therefore I take pleasure in infirmities, in re-

proaches, in necessities, in persecutions, in distresses for Christ's sake: for when I am weak, then am I strong.

Matthew 5:10 Blessed *are* they which are persecuted for righteousness' sake: for theirs is the kingdom of heaven.

I watched Ministries be destroyed before my eyes, and at the time, I didn't realize that I had the power inside of me to stand, pray, and come against the enemy. There was a grace upon me during this time, but a year later I had a down time. It was only then that I fully began to grasp what standing for that ministry meant. I needed some time to heal.

I bring up this story not so that I can be glorified, but so that people can realize that the devil will try to come into a ministry and destroy it from the inside. If he's given an opening, he'll take it. You must be intercessors. Be watchman on the wall of the ministries.

Keep a cool head. Stay alert. The Devil is poised to pounce, and would like nothing better than to catch you napping. Keep your guard up. You're not the only ones plunged into these hard times. It's the same with Christians all over the world. So keep a firm grip on the faith. The suffering won't last forever. It won't be long before this generous God who has great plans for us in Christ—eternal and glorious plans they are!—will have you put together and on your feet for good. He gets the last word; yes, he does (1 Peter 5:8 MSG).

Don't give the devil room to come into your churches and friendships. Don't give him the room to mess with what God has given you. The Acts church had people coming into it by the hundreds and thousands.

Acts 2:47 Praising God, and having favour with all the people. And the Lord added to the church daily such as should be saved.

The Acts church wasn't just focused on getting their church together. They were taking the message of Jesus Christ out into the streets. These people were changing their cities, and ultimately the Gospel went out into the world. It wasn't like as soon as the Holy Spirit came, they all decided who was going to run the kid's department musical. There is nothing wrong with things like that, but I'm saying ministry wasn't all about departments. They took the Gospel to the street.

When I was a kid, I remember trying to invite children to a church function and being told that people who didn't go to our church weren't invited, because a particular person wanted the function to stay "in house" to "build" the church's departments. I understand what they were saying. It was this person's place to make that decision, but we have to stop being so focused on building our church and be more focused on building the community who sees the church and wants to be a part of it. We're laboring for His Kingdom, not our own.

If we want to drive the spirit of Balaam out of the Church, we have to come down from our high and lofty places as churches and begin to reach out to those around us. The Acts church took care of each other.

And when they had prayed, the place was shaken where they were assembled together; and they were all filled with the Holy Ghost, and they spoke the word of God with boldness. And the multitude of them that believed were of one heart and of one soul: neither said any of them that there be things which he possessed was his own; but they had all things common.

Acts 4:31-37 And when they had prayed, the place was shaken where they were assembled together; and they were all filled with the Holy Ghost, and they spake the word of God with boldness. And the multitude of them that believed were of one heart and of one soul: neither said any *of them* that ought of the things which he possessed was his own; but they had all things common. And with great power gave the apostles witness of the resurrection of the Lord Jesus: and great grace was upon them all. Neither was there any among them that lacked: for as many as were possessors of lands or houses sold them, and brought the prices of the things that were sold, And laid *them* down at the apostles' feet: and distribution was made unto every man according as he had need. And Joses, who by the apostles was surnamed Barnabas, (which is, being interpreted, The son of consolation,) a Levite, *and* of the country of Cyprus, Having land, sold *it,* and brought the money, and laid *it* at the apostles' feet.

I am not about to say it's wrong for churches to have people who have more money than others. I am not about to claim God is saying that it's wrong to have excess. That's communistic, and if you think this way, you're missing the point. The church took care of each other. They brought what they had to the church, and all the needs were met. How can we relate to that in today's world?

I've had the privilege of being part of apostolic giving services, and I have to say they're awesome. In the past God used to randomly feel that a particular service would be set aside for apostolic giving, and the night would always bring blessings to people. Basically the premise of apostolic giving is that people ask God if there is anything they need to give, and when it's time they say it. If there is a person who needs that item, they say they have need of it. I've been in services where cars, furniture, money for gas, and other items were given. If you have kids a certain age, look around your church and pray to find a family with kid's right behind your children's ages. Instead of throwing out you kid's old clothes, maybe you could bless a family who could really use them. What about the same thing with other items? When you are in the church, stay open for the Lord to tell you if you have anything you can do to bless your brothers and sisters. If they don't have a lawnmower, then go mow their grass. Do for others what you would want them to do for you. If someone needs a ride and you don't have a problem with that, then give it to them. It's really fun when you do things anonymously. When you do something for someone else, don't call attention to yourself. You've seen them in action, I'm sure—'play-actors' I call them—treating prayer meeting and street corner alike as a stage, acting compassionate as long as someone is watching, playing to the crowds. They get applause, true, but that's all they get. When you help someone out, don't think about how it looks. Just do it—quietly and unobtrusively. That is the way your God, who conceived you in love, working behind the scenes, helps you out (Matthew 6:2-4 MSG).

Just start helping the people around you who need help. You might have to start being a good family member before others start treating you like one. You reap in the Kingdom what you sow. I got the chance to bless someone with a car once. Then a few years ago, we were in need of a car and someone blessed us with one. Apostolic giving really works! It's not always about what you'll get out of it, but being a blessing to others will give you more fulfillment in your local church body than you realize.

And the Lord said unto Cain, Where is Abel thy brother? And he said, I know not: Am I my brother's keeper? (Genesis 4:9 KJV)

It's up to us to help them in any way we can. Again, I'm not saying to be a doormat, but if I have two sandwiches and you have none, then I need to bless you with a free lunch. That's becoming a family.

Sadly, I've heard too many people in the Church say that if someone is going through something and they're still struggling then, well, "It's up to them. I guess their faith isn't strong enough." That is a lie from the pits of hell. Jesus laid hands on people whose faith wasn't quite there.

I walked through some physical battles back in 2000. I will be the first person to tell you my faith just wasn't built up in the area of physical healing the way it should have been. When the doctors starting telling me that I had to accept the fact that this physical issue was there or that I would have to go on medication—and began listing all their negativity, which is contrary to what I know God says about healing and what I knew the Lord had spoken over my life—I panicked. It's easy to talk about faith, but when you walk through a serious circumstance, it's also easy to lose your cool. I wasn't the mighty man of faith I thought I was. My faith had become like melted Jell-O at my feet. I refused to let me believe what the doctors and the circumstances were telling me. In fact, he refused so strongly that I had to call him on the phone every day for six months throughout this process. Every day, he'd talk to me and pray with me.

This is not common in the Body of Christ. Too many of us are so caught up in our own worlds that we'd barely do this for someone once. I had some people that wouldn't let me fall when my flesh was failing. When the physical symptoms started to change and the doctor's reports changed, it came as no surprise to him. Today all symptoms but one have gone, and even that symptom has continued to get better than what it was. In Jesus name I believe that one is changing, and one day I will see the full manifestation. God is a supernatural God. It gets Him excited when He gets to show off in that way. But in these kinds of areas, sometimes people just need someone there to encourage them and lift them up.

In Exodus 17 is a story about a battle in which, as long as Moses arms were lifted up, the Israelites were winning. But Moses' arms got tired. Of course they did. Anyone's arms would get tired staying up in the air for an extended period of time. So Aaron and Hur helped keep Moses' arms up. Eventually the battle was won. There are times in life when people need you to hold up their arms while they're going through a rough season. I needed Pastor Arthur's help with what I walked through. It was too much for me to handle on my own. He loved me enough to refuse to let me fail. Will you do that for those around you when they're hurting? Or will you walk by and make yourself feel better by just saying, "I guess they just don't have the faith to be healed." They need your help through prayer, fasting, encouragement, and listening. They don't need your condemnation.

This point can be best illustrated by the story in Luke 5:17-26. There was a paralyzed man whose friends picked him up on a mat to take him to Jesus. They were sure Jesus could heal him, but when they showed up on the scene, there was no room for them to get to Jesus. They were so convinced that Jesus could heal their friend that they tore a hole in the house where Jesus was and lowered their friend down the hole just to get him to Jesus. In verse 20 it says that, when Jesus saw their faith, He said, "Friend, your sins are forgiven." Those friends loved that man enough to refuse to give up on him. They went out of their way to get him to his healing and his destiny. Now, eventually it is up to the man who gets healed, as far as whether he will grab hold of what Jesus said or stay on his mat. Later in the passage, Jesus tells him to get up and walk. This man who was paralyzed did, and he was healed! But it was the faith of the friends who got him to the place to receive his healing. He had been paralyzed. He needed help!

We can't rely all the time on someone else's faith, because ultimately it comes down to us and God. But in that situation, I am convinced that, if others had not carried me like he did in those months, I would have never gotten my feet back underneath me to believe.

The entire testimony is quite miraculous, and eventually I did have to learn to stand on my own with God, but until I got to that point, I was carried there.

We have to do those kinds of things for our brothers and sisters in the Lord. We have to get a revelation that we are their keepers. If they're struggling, call them. Pray for them. If they need groceries and you can bless them, then do so. Be a blessing to the world around you!

Denominations often can and do create boundaries within the Body of Christ. This has always been a unique revelation in my life which I seek to bring to the Body of Christ.

I bring up all of this denominational stuff to say this—the Body of Christ keeps each other segregated by too many denominational walls and labels. It's like a shield that the Christian carries in their wallet. "I go to such and such a church." I just don't understand that. I guess Paul didn't either.

I have a serious concern to bring up with you, my friends, using the authority of Jesus, our Master. I'll put it as urgently as I can: You must get along with each other. You must learn to be considerate of one another, cultivating a life in common.

We have to stop hiding behind our denominational walls. Paul, in this Scripture, is getting annoyed at the early church for doing this same thing. "I'm with so-and-so," and, "I follow so-and-so's teaching." The bottom line is, do you follow Jesus? Is Jesus your cornerstone? Is the Bible your foundation? That's all that matters in this question. Everything else, while important, can't be used to cause strife and division. Do I think everyone should have an infilling of the Holy Spirit? Absolutely! It's like putting the light on in a room. By the blood of Jesus, you get into the room, but the Spirit turns the light on. I believe in speaking in tongues and flowing in the gifts, but if you don't, fighting over it isn't getting souls out of hell—it's just fighting over it. We need to strive to be at peace with each other, even if we don't agree on every little thing.

For as the body is one, and hath many members, and all the members of that one body, being many, are one body: so also is Christ. For by one Spirit are we all baptized into one body, whether we be Jews or Gentiles, whether we be bond or free; and have been all made to drink into one Spirit.

For the body is not one member, but many. If the foot shall say, Because I am not the hand, I am not of the body; is it therefore not of the body? And if the ear shall say, Because I am not the eye, I am not of the body; is it therefore not of the body? If the whole body were an eye, where were the hearing? If the whole were hearing, where were the smelling? But now hath God set the members every one of them in the body, as it hath pleased Him. And if they were all one member, where were the body?

But now are they many members, yet but one body. And the eye cannot say unto the hand, I have no need of thee: nor again the head to the feet, I have no need of you. Nay, much more those members of the body, which seem to be more feeble, are necessary: and those members of the body, which we think to be less honorable, upon these we bestow more abundant honor; and our uncommon parts have more abundant beauty. For our comely parts have no need: but God hath tempered the body together, having given more abundant honor to that part which lacked. That there should be no schism in the body; but that the members should have the same care one for another. And whether one member suffer, all the members suffer with it; or one member be honored, all the members rejoice with it.

Now ye are the body of Christ, and members in particular. And God hath set some in the church, first apostles, secondarily prophets, thirdly teachers, after that miracles, then gifts of healings, helps, governments, diversities of tongues. Are all apostles? are all prophets? are all teachers? are all workers of miracles? Have all the gifts of healing? do all speak with tongues? do all interpret? But covet earnestly the best gifts: and yet shew I unto you a more excellent way (1 Corinthians 12:12-31 KJV).

One church may be called to be a foot and another an eye. It's their job to be the best foot and eye they can be in the Body of Christ. What I've seen is that we sit around in our high and lofty chairs, thinking we're so much better than another church because we have a revelation about some things and they don't. We can't make an arm be an ear. That's ludicrous. You have to be the part you're called to be in the Body. I've always joked that I was the sparkle in the Bride of Christ's eye. I recently heard a dear friend of mine, who is a church secretary, saying that she's the bowels of the church because she makes it go on time.

Whatever you are, be that. But you can't think that you're any better than another part. When one cell gets out of whack in your physical body, what happens? It can cause pain or cancer. It's the same in the church. Cells are thinking they'd be better at being a big toe. Last week I saw a big toe trying to be a pinkie finger. Really, it's no wonder the people in the world think we look crazy.

If you don't feel that a church like the one I go to is for you, then fine. I guess it's fine to call yourself a denomination too, but you can't wear that like a label or badge. You can't hide behind it. I was around a man once who got really annoyed with me because he kept trying to label the denomination I was, and when he couldn't, it ticked him off. If people can label you, they will try to control you by that label. Greatly to the aggravation of some folks, when people ask me what "religion" I am, I always say I'm a Christian. I am a Christ follower, in a relationship with God—a tongue-talking, Spirit-filled child of the living King. Most of the time, they don't want to know what religion I am, they want to know what denomination I am. Then they stumble around again and ask me my religion, and again I respond, "I am a Christian." It's time denominational walls come down and allow us to be the Body of Christ. I am a Christian. Luther, Calvin, and Wesley were all mighty men of God, but I don't wear their label. I wear the label of Christ.

So now that you've read this book and seen the sad fact that the spirit of Balaam has run rampant through the Church, what do you do now?

First, you pray! You pray that God would show you how you can make a difference in your community and in your church. Ask the Lord to reveal to you the times when you've missed it. Some of you, as you're reading this now, are seeing images pass before your eyes in your memory, and you know you've missed it in some areas.

Next, you repent! Repentance is not saying to God, "Sure God, I'm sorry!" Repentance is doing a 180-degree turn in the opposite direction. Repentance is a constant choice that you will not let the spirit of Balaam have your life. Declare now that the boundaries are set and that you and your church are off-limits to the spirit of Balaam. You do not want to be known as a no-nothing person. You want to create a legacy in the Kingdom of God. Begin to make yourself care about those around you. Don't just read this book and think, "Oh, well, nice revelation." Do something about it! Recognize that it's an issue. The spirit of Balaam for years has been the issue in the Church that no one wants to talk about, but now it's time to address it. It's time to stop trying to hide it and, instead, to realize it's there so we can get it out. Let's pour ourselves into the ones God puts around us. Let's make a difference on this earth. Let's be ready for Jesus' return.

Last, get ready! Change will come. Unity will come. You must be ready for it. You must shake off your ankle weights of the past. It's okay because Jesus is in you. You're running the race He has set before you. Don't be scared, be excited! These are awesome times to be in the Kingdom of God. Something is moving, like a rumbling in the spirit realm. God is getting ready to do such exciting things in His Church.

We must be ready. We must stop compromising what the Word of God says and get ready. We must stop trying to fit in with the world and be separate. "Wherefore come out from among them, and be ye separate, saith the Lord" (2 Corinthians 6:17a KJV). Be different from the world. Let them see that there is a moving and living God on the inside of you. Then they will want what you have! Be a family of God. Work as a team. Walk in unity. Walk in His love.

Please, I am begging you—we need your help in the Church. Don't be part of the problem any longer. Choose to be a blessing and not a curse.

Choose to push out the spirit of Balaam. Don't be known as a no-nothing person, but be a something person. Be a person with sustenance! Come join us as we impact the world for His glory!

7

~

Implementing and Sharing Vision

Isa 55:11 So shall my word be that goeth forth out of my mouth: it shall not return unto me void, but it shall accomplish that which I please, and it shall prosper *in the thing* whereto I sent it.

When vision moves from consolidation there is an acceleration that leads to *implementation* i.e. the vision is put into effect for the purpose for which God planned. Big vision requires apostolic leadership to set a course for the future and stay on target by being led by the Spirit of wisdom and revelation. As vision is implemented and infrastructure formed you will be enabled to cast (share) vision, identify partnership, determine tasks, write job descriptions, put policies and procedures in place, appoint leaders to execute duties and assign spheres of responsibility. It is clear than when people know what they are expected to do, they make a better job of doing it than when they are unsure.

Infrastructure n. the basic physical and organizational structures (e.g. buildings, roads, power supplies) needed for the operation of a society or enterprise. I've discovered that both strategy and infrastructure normally come quickly after the commitment and character testing stages. Jesus left the wilderness full of the power of the Holy Spirit and began preaching and ministering. An appointed spiritual wilderness that is part of vision preparation will always be followed by a release of power anointing that acts as a catalyst to release the next stage of the policies, procedures and people needed in partnership to fulfill the vision. *A policy* is a course or principle of action adopted or proposed by an organization or individual. A *procedure* is an established or official way of doing something or a series of actions conducted in a certain order or manner. When building infrastructure I always ask myself five simple questions:

1. What is it I want to accomplish?

This focuses me on my vision and the task in hand and helps me to set clear aims and objectives. I have an overall vision and to implement it I need to identify strategic/tactical steps that will enable me to fulfill the mandate.

2. When does it need to be done by?

Fixing an approximate time frame helps me to establish a working time-line for vision execution. I usually have to review my time-line on a regular basis. One mistake I have made in the past is not allowing enough time to execute various aspects of vision implementation.

3. Who are the people who will help me to achieve my goals?

Looking at your current people resource base is essential to determine what skills you can presently access to accomplish vision. A quick review will identify any areas of need and help in planning for the future. Asking the "who" question also helps me to plan how I might bring potential partners on board. "Who?" is a key networking question and networking is an important element of vision implementation.

4. How am I going to do this?

Asking yourself how you are actually going to achieve your vision will shape your policies and procedures for the present and the future. I have found grappling in prayer and in action with the "how to" of vision becomes catalytic in moving vision from an 'abstract' idea to an actual reality. Take your time on this stage and don't be tempted to fast track.

5. Where is the task going to be accomplished?

Asking myself this question helps me to decide on where "base camp" should be; there has to be a central hub from which communications flow and which serves as an operational base.

The answers to these five questions will enable me to formulate a God-given plan and a divinely inspired plan is essential if one is to build to a heavenly blue print.

Having been pruned, refined and polished you are now prepared as the primary vision carrier to communicate your vision to others! This should be done in a clear, concise manner. As vision is shared the Holy Spirit ignites a God-given desire in other people to become *'metochos'* i.e. partakers, partners, collaborators with you in the vision. These appointed partners become 'secondary vision carriers'. The primary vision carrier is responsible for overseeing the overall vision. Partners release provision to the vision. Apostle Paul states that we have been enriched in every way and we do not lack any spiritual gift! *1 Corinthians 1:5-7*

After the initial prayer and inquiry stage I was able to put together a draft timescale for the various aspects of the vision.

From Scripture we note how Jesus calls His disciples one by one in a personal encounter. As He draws us to Himself, some are called to be fore-runners and pioneers blazing a trail and setting a path for others to walk upon; we might say that such a person is designated as a primary visionary or vision carrier.

When Jesus joins His heart with that of a primary visionary and births vision within that person, an inner circle is formed through which Kingdom vision will be released.

We might describe this as a wheel of momentum, with Jesus as the central hub. Wheels cause things to move forward and momentum is necessary to move vision forward.

Prophet Ezekiel (Ezekiel 1) paints a picture of a wheel within a wheel, and apostolic pioneering ministry is built on this principle with Jesus at the core. Intimacy with God releases revelation and vision is birthed in the heart of the believer. Partnering with heaven sets destiny in motion on the earth.

The primary visionary reaches out to potential vision supporters/

partners the primary visionary shares their God-given vision and this ignites the vision in other people's hearts. Sharing vision works on the principle of Isaiah 55:10- 11: when God's 'word' i.e. the vision seeds are shared with others (cast abroad) they do not return to Him empty and they accomplish what God desires for them in achievement of the purpose for which they were sent. Primary Visionary Shares Vision with Potential Vision Partners a seed needs somewhere to be planted and God plants His vision seed in other hearts as the word goes forth, providing seed for the sower and bread for the hungry. New supporters/partners may be described as 1st generation partners and/or secondary visionary carriers. When others embrace the vision and come on board as partners to the vision and values communicated by the primary visionary, a second relational link is made, which continues to act like a wheel to move things forward from vision consolidation stage to vision implementation.

These secondary vision supporters/partners communicate with others and in so doing create 2nd, 3rd, 4th and subsequent generations of vision supporters/ partners. Such multiplication enables sharing of resource and vision is carried forward under the direction and inspiration of the Holy Spirit. Viewing partnership as a multiplication process promotes a healthy environment in which to relate and build Kingdom vision together rather than a hierarchical structure that limits people's creativity and potential to invest and add to the original vision remit. When people are valued and treated as equal partners in vision fulfilment they will naturally take on a sense of ownership of the vision and as an outflow will reach out to those in their circles of relationship and bring more partners on board as vision continues to be shared. 2nd Generation Partnership Multiplication Sharing Vision causes Mobilisation. Mobilisation is to prepare and organise troops for active service and/or organize people (or resources) for a particular task. Momentum is a natural outflow of mobilisation. Momentum is the impetus gained by movement or progress. One can confidently expect acceleration of vision as partners are mobilised and come on board.

With momentum comes acceleration; Accelerate means to begin to move more quickly increasing in rate, amount or extent. In physics it means to undergo a chance in velocity; velocity being the speed at which something is given direction.

With acceleration the vision begins to be outworked = implementation. Implementation means to put into effect.

In implementing vision I learned that a good leader is a caring leader and will show pastoral oversight for those in their charge.

Apostle Paul wrote, *"Even though you have 10,000 guardians in Christ, you do not have many fathers, for in Christ Jesus I became your father through the gospel." 1 Corinthians 4: 5*

Jesus valued people over programs and so must we. Details and duties are important but not at the expense of people. As a leader we must be willing to invest in and develop the people God sends to partner with us in vision. Leadership is an incredible privilege and we must steward this privilege with humility, compassion, righteousness and grace.

Don't be afraid to process regularly and meet with your advisors, your team and make ongoing assessments. A wise leader will face issues and find a way to resolve them. Don't be tempted to ignore problems – they won't go away! What were the original aims? Are the tactical steps working? Is vision being implemented? What changes (if any) need to be made? Create opportunities for regular review and feedback from your team members and partners and pray for and with them on an on-going basis. He also entrusts the responsibility of stewardship of leadership to you and whilst once must make room for the gifting of others, one must not allow others to usurp the God-given authority to lead Kingdom vision.

As a visionary leader you will have to overcome fear but don't give in - intimidation will come but more important God will give you strategy and courage to overcome. Nehemiah faced many enemies but the work continued.

In the face of adversity Nehemiah prayed, *"Now Lord, strengthen our hands!"*

Apostolic anointing is a laboring anointing and visionary leaders are not lazy people they model hard work, diligence and dedication and as a result can inspire others to do the same.

8

~

In Spirit and In Truth

John 4:24 God *is* a Spirit: and they that worship him must worship *him* in spirit and in truth.

When we pray in the Spirit, in our heavenly language, demons do not understand because we are speaking mysteries to God.

Psalms 150:6 states, *"Let everything that has breath, Praise the Lord...."*

How can people praise the Lord, exactly? Well, they can praise the Lord in their own language by using God's universal tongue. I know many believers do not believe that speaking in tongues is for today, but they speak in a tongue, nevertheless. Some Bible scholars and leaders from other denominations might not believe in speaking in tongues, declaring it was only for the early church, yet they speak in a tongue. His Father's name. *Yahushua* is also a derivative of the name Joshua.

John 5:43 I am come in my Father's name, and ye receive me not: if another shall come in his own name, him ye will receive.

He is worthy to be praised, no matter what country, culture, barrier, or background we can think of; God will break the backs of demons and break down any walls that try to counter Him. He will make sure that every praise, prayer, and cry of every spirit who worships Him will reach His ear when it is coming from a heart that is untainted and reverent. He is not impressed with eloquent speech or how sophisticatedly we can put words together in prayer, but with how real our hearts of compassion are toward Him. God is searching for pure hearts that desire to serve with no negative motives involved. When we have compassion to serve, we are laying down the very fundamental nature of who we are. Moreover, we hit a point of wanting to surrender ourselves, no matter the cost, because of who we are in Christ. Our consecrated spirits in us have to connect with who God is. Intricately, our spirits have to be knitted together with the will of the Father.

We must be people of integrity and remain true to God and our leaders. Continue to be the peacemaker when all else is crumbling and falling apart. In all that you do in work or deed, continue to fight against having a mindset of complaining or murmuring (see Philippians 2:14). Do not encourage it by listening to the mess that comes out of the mouths of other people. Walk in the Spirit and in the truth (see John 14:6). Travel with people you can trust. You cannot inform everyone of all your personal secrets, issues, desires, visions, and plans. Did you know that it takes anointing, ability, power, and authority to be able to handle your mess? This is true not only for a person's ability to hear your troubles, but also the ability to help you develop a blueprint in your mind for how to deal with your issues. There are people who are not able to handle it; it will do more damage than good—occasionally. At other times, if you are not careful and you confess private information about yourself to people you thought you could trust, you may find yourself the subject of ridicule and gossip. This is a perfect example of the importance of discerning between your "associates" and those you call your "friends." Not everyone in your circle of influence will be compassionate about your personal matters; sharing with such people will only bring unnecessary contention and distress into your life. Be in constant prayer and surround yourself with anointed people of God who can facilitate in the time of need and encourage you whenever you need aid. You need that life support to help you breathe when the enemy is seeking to strangle your dreams and choke your visions right out of your heart and spirit. Don't just rebuke when the enemy comes against you like a flood, but expel, destroy, repel, and resist him in the name of Jesus. And God will raise that standard for you and with you. He will stand triumphantly, and so will you in the name of the Lord Jesus! Watch and pray always. As I said earlier, a "watchman" is considered a prophet in the Old Testament, but in other cases, such as these, it can mean to watch out for yourself and others in the spirit. Be wise as a serpent and yet gentle as a dove. Fight back in the spirit, and take back what the enemy has stolen from you; he has done enough after all these years of stealing, beating you down, and taking what never belonged to him in the first place. I had to fight hard to get back what I had allowed the devil to take from me. Satan steals your visions, destroys your spirit, and devours your dreams—but only if you are unaware of the enemy's devices, tactics, and deceptions. You must understand that the enemy is very real and conniving, and he plays for keeps, with the goal of making sure your future is dark, cold, and unbearable. There are Christians who state that Jesus is their love, but they are wolves in sheep's clothing. And they will steal from you if you let them.

Jesus knew that His image-bearers would not imagine the fact that a loving God could create such a horrific place of torment for anyone but the devil and his angels. I know that hell exists, not only because the holy men of God wrote about it in the Bible, but because I was actually allowed to come out of my body, experiencing the spirit realm firsthand. I would like to assure you hell is a real and tangible place in the center of the earth, as recorded in the Scriptures.

Matthew 12:40 For as Jonas was three days and three nights in the whale's belly; so shall the Son of man be three days and three nights in the heart of the earth.

John 2:1, 2 Then Jonah prayed unto the LORD his God out of the fish's belly, And said, I cried by reason of mine affliction unto the LORD, and he heard me; out of the belly of hell cried I, *and* thou heardest my voice.

John 2:4-7 Then I said, I am cast out of thy sight; yet I will look again toward thy holy temple. The waters compassed me about, *even* to the soul: the depth closed me round about, the weeds were wrapped about my head. I went down to the bottoms of the mountains; the earth with her bars *was* about me for ever: yet hast thou brought up my life from corruption, O LORD my God. When my soul fainted within me I remembered the LORD: and my prayer came in unto thee, into thine holy temple.

Ephesians 4:8-10 Wherefore he saith, When he ascended up on high, he led captivity captive, and gave gifts unto men. (Now that he ascended, what is it but that he also descended first into the lower parts of the earth? He that descended is the same also that ascended up far above all heavens, that he might fill all things.)

You will not find mountains or an earth with bars inside of a whale's stomach; Jonah died in the belly of the whale, which was symbolic, a parallel between Jesus and Jonah contrasting Jesus' death with Jonah's. No human can survive living in a stomach full of acid. (Stomach acid will severely burn skin. The pH level is 1-2, the same as hydrochloric acid.) Jonah's soul started to descend, and as he was descending, he saw mountains, as well as the bars in hell, appearing in front of him. Jonah prayed and repented to God, and the Lord heard his plea, causing the whale to vomit him out onto dry land. My point is, hell is an actual place with fire, fear, and undying hopelessness with no anticipation of ever getting out! Unfortunately, repentance does not exist for those who have died in their sins; hell becomes their eternal home. While we are yet alive, we can make the decision to accept Christ so we don't send ourselves to hell forever. We choose a path—either to die twice or to live twice. If we include physical death, it's really dying three times if we are in sin. According to Hebrews and Revelation (see Hebrews 9:27; Revelations 2:11), sinners will die a natural death once and spiritual death twice. Born-again believers will live twice, unless they experience natural death on earth. Let me explain: Sinners will die a natural death once on earth and then die a second time when placed in hades. Jesus said He is going to take hades and cast it into the lake of fire, which is considered hell—the third death (see Revelations 20:14). When the New Testament was written in the Greek, the English translators replaced the word *hades* with *hell,* when in true essence *gehenna* should be translated *hell* in the Gospels (see Matthews 10:28; Revelations 20:14). Revelation is only speaking about spiritual death. Considering the possibility of a "second death," which path will we choose?

1. **The Sinners/Backsliders Path:** A sinner dies physically, *once*. Then the sinner dies a *second* time spiritually and is sent to hades/ hell. Then the sinner dies a *third* time after the Great White Throne Judgment, which is a more horrible death then the second because the sinner is sent into the lake of fire to be tormented in the same place as the devil and his angels.

2. **Path of the Child of God:** Two paths are available to the child of God. On Path 1, the saint lives physically *once* (is raptured) and then lives again for all eternity (thus, the saint lives *twice*). On Path 2, the saint dies physically *once* (is not raptured) and then lives again for all eternity (thus, the saint dies once and then lives again). According to tradition, hades or hell—whichever we feel most comfortable using—is considered to be like sweating in a very, very hot sauna. When the sinner is placed into the lake of fire, with the devil and his angels, that same sinner will be in the exact location suffering torment in agony and torture for all eternity because of rejecting Christ as Lord and Savior. This is one of the main reasons satan and his demons are trying very hard to get us back into sin and our old ways. His goal is to keep us where we are, making sure we don't get right with God; he wants our eternal future to be the same as his. Regrettably, there are thousands of Christians who do not believe there is a devil or a literal hell. I believe if there was no hell then Jesus would have never revealed it in the Scriptures. Here are just a few of the passages in the Bible about hell:

Mark 9:43-48 And if thy hand offend thee, cut it off: it is better for thee to enter into life maimed, than having two hands to go into hell, into the fire that never shall be quenched: Where their worm dieth not, and the fire is not quenched. And if thy foot offend thee, cut it off: it is better for thee to enter halt into life, than having two feet to be cast into hell, into the fire that never shall be quenched: Where their worm dieth not, and the fire is not quenched. And if thine eye offend thee, pluck it out:

it is better for thee to enter into the kingdom of God with one eye, than having two eyes to be cast into hell fire: Where their worm dieth not, and the fire is not quenched.

Ezekiel 18:4 Behold, all souls are mine; as the soul of the father, so also the soul of the son is mine: the soul that sinneth, it shall die.

Hebrews 9:27 And as it is appointed unto men once to die, but after this the judgment:

Job 7:1 *Is there* not an appointed time to man upon earth? *are not* his days also like the days of an hireling?

Matthew 10:28 And fear not them which kill the body, but are not able to kill the soul: but rather fear him which is able to destroy both soul and body in hell.

9

Kingdom FOUNDATION

Unless the Lord builds the house, its builders labour in vain. Psalm 127:1

Building is part of apostolic ministry function and is carried out through the anointing of grace given to apostolic leaders by the Holy Spirit. Apostle Paul wrote to the church in Corinth stressing how important it was to build by grace and on the foundation of Christ alone:

"By the grace God has given me, I laid a foundation as an expert builder and someone else is building on it. But each one should be careful how he builds. For no one can lay any foundation other than the one already laid, which is Jesus Christ." 1 Corinthians 3:10

Apostle Paul teaches that God's household is built upon the foundations of the apostles and prophets, with Christ Jesus himself as the chief cornerstone. In Christ we are all joined together and are being build together to become a dwelling place in which God lives by His Spirit. (*Ephesians 2:20*) When we build we must chart a course for the future with apostolic wisdom and prophetic insight. We cannot build without a plan from God. Apostles and apostolic visionary leaders receive blue prints and may be described as "pattern makers" (*Philippians 3:17*)

As you exercise faith and surrender in obedience to God's call on your life you will walk in His unprecedented favor. It has been my experience that the gift of God in you will make room for your vision and your vision will make room for the gift of God in you.

As a visionary leader God will enable you to see the 'big picture.' i.e. where you are now and where you need to be in the future. Seeing through a long-term lens will release the divine blue print and strategy at the appointed time. As the leader of a God-given dream there may be times when only you can see what lies ahead and it is your responsibility to ensure that the vision stays on track and in step with God's time line. He will show you how to establish His plans and purposes at the pre-ordained and appointed time.

Within every God-given visionary leader is the capacity to hear from God in order to comprehend and competently fulfill vision. God grants His leaders wisdom and discernment to know how, when and what decisions should be made. Because the Lord had sovereignly appointed me for the task He also graced me with the wisdom to know what to do and when to do it.

Nehemiah was an apostolic builder, whom God assigned to rebuild the wall of Jerusalem. He was a reformer and a pioneer and did something that no-one else had ever done before him. It was essential that he stayed close to the heart of God during every step of his vision. Visionary leaders are pioneer builders and as we study the life of Nehemiah we discover it is an invaluable resource and helps us to understand the various stages of vision including how to overcome enemy opposition through responsive counterstrategy. Apostolic pioneers have the tenacity, patience and authority to penetrate new territory, overcome hostile enemy and establish, advance and maintain God's Kingdom.

The only way vision can be fully achieved is when God's appointed leader surrenders in totality to Christ's sovereign ruler ship in his/her life. Preparation and pruning of my heart was a foundational part of being made ready for dependability of what God had for me. Pioneering building in unknown territory should only be carried out in the grace and wisdom that comes from complete God-reliance and trusting His ability to fulfil His promises in and to us.

Staying close to Jesus in covenant relationship releases His authority in our lives. Godly leaders must come to an experiential understanding that intimacy with Christ and leading sacrificial lifestyles that emulate the Master release His anointing and authority in us and through us. My relationship with Jesus deepened throughout the three years of spearheading the Revival vision and when things got difficult (as often happens in the course of our faith journey) my relationship with God was the core source of my on-going inspiration and ability to overcome obstacles.

As you lay the foundation for the vision to be outworked God will give you, as His primary vision carrier, the ability to identify achievable time lines and to clarify what the main vision aims and objectives are. I consulted with a number of other leaders in the initial stages to review my original thoughts and was very happy to have their input.

During the foundation stage of vision God confronts us with reality of the level of involvement and commitment required from us in order for vision to be accomplished. I have found it is helpful to review past experience alongside of present priorities in order to establish potential for future commitment. I counted the cost of pursuing the dream and God gave me grace and courage to say 'yes' to the new faith adventure He placed before me.

Generally, I have to have a dream burning in me before I can exercise faith for infrastructure. Although you may not have policy and procedure in the early days, God will release infrastructure to you as you press in and pray and seek understanding of the vision He has entrusted to you.

I've discovered that God increases our ability to network and develop strategic Kingdom alliances during foundation stage and throughout fulfilment of vision. Networking assists in mobilization and mobilization is a necessary part of vision implementation. During Revivals God surprised me with the amazing doors of favor He opened with ministries, on TV and in radio.

It is a good idea to share your vision with other leaders with whom you have relationship and look for a consensus of agreement within your Kingdom spheres of influence. Don't forget to share your vision with your spouse – having the support of your husband or wife is the best way to move vision forward.

No leader should be isolated and having ministerial friends to relate with and be accountable to is a Kingdom principle, for instance the original apostles had true friendships with each other and met regularly (e.g. the Council of Jerusalem) for input and consultation on various church matters. Accountability is protection and helps to keep us grounded and supported by others who help us to see our "blind spots." A *blind spot* is simply an area where a person's view is obstructed. We need each other's perspective to help build the bigger picture.

10

~

Partnership and Multiplication

Luke 5:7 And they beckoned unto *their* partners, which were in the other ship, that they should come and help them. And they came, and filled both the ships, so that they began to sink.

As we consider the outworking of apostolic global vision it is evident that a single church, ministry, organization or business entrepreneur cannot fulfill their mandate without the support that comes through God-appointed partnership.

The saving grace of our Lord Jesus Christ is not just for the moment of our personal salvation. God's grace is also given in order that He can reach whole communities and see them transformed by His love and the message of the Kingdom outworked in Godly vision. This requires commitment, co-operation and collaboration with the Holy Spirit and with those with whom we work in Spirit-led relationship.

Collaborate 1. Work jointly on an activity or project 2. Co-operate traitorously with an enemy

Commitment n. 1. the state or quality of being dedicated to a cause or policy; a pledge or undertaking

Co-operate v. work towards the same end; assist someone or comply with their requests In the context of our Kingdom calling:

• There is a place for each person's gifting. Each must take up their appointed 'position' in God's army.

• There is a need for release of resources in order for vision to be fulfilled. This may take the form of prayer, contacts, talent, gift, calling, finances, serving, giving of time etc.

• Apostolic oversight is important to ensure equality and right stewardship. Working with five-fold ministry teams (apostle, prophet, evangelist, pastor, and teacher) will ensure that the body is trained and equipped and brought to maturity in Christ at the same time as vision is fulfilled. (see *Ephesians 4*)

Jesus underlined the two most important commands of all during His earthly life. The first is to love God with all our hearts, soul, mind and strength; the second is to love our neighbor as we love our self. We are mandated to love. This is our commanded mission, our message and our mantle. All vision and mission partnership must embody these values. The Apostle Paul, in his letter to Philemon, appealed on the basis of love to his hearers that they would receive Onesimus as his son and a partner in the faith. Similarly, when Paul spoke of Titus to the Philippians he was keen that they would understand that his representative shared the heart of God with them.

The Kingdom of God is all about multiplication. Jesus said, "*Go and make disciples*" and this speaks of mandated increase. Partnership in vision enables the Kingdom to advance under the authority, power and love of Christ. Partnership with heaven is not a peripheral activity; it is an essential part of our commission on earth.

Luke 5:1-4 And it came to pass, that, as the people pressed upon him to hear the word of God, he stood by the lake of Gennesaret, And saw two ships standing by the lake: but the fishermen were gone out of them, and were washing *their* nets. And he entered into one of the ships, which was Simon's, and prayed him that he would thrust out a little from the land. And he sat down, and taught the people out of the ship. Now when he had left speaking, he said unto Simon, Launch out into the deep, and let down your nets for a draught.

Jesus' priority was obedience to His Father and to reaching the lost, preaching the Kingdom and making disciples. The Lord taught about the

Kingdom of God everywhere He went. The context of our call to partnership with heaven and each other is no different today. We are to go into all nations and to make disciples and we do so by preaching, teaching and demonstrating the Gospel message of the Kingdom, healing the sick, cleansing the lepers, delivering the demonized and raising the dead.

Despite the fact that Jesus was surrounded by a large crowd He didn't fail to notice that there were two boats by the lake side. When we look through God's eyes we will also see the divine potential for the miracle manifestation of God's glory all around us. Jesus was a pioneer. Pioneers are those who are willing to go ahead and make a way for others to follow; every visionary leader is a pioneer. Pioneers have patience and endurance to contend till breakthrough is evident.

One boat was left by the water's edge, whilst Jesus instructed Simon to step into the second boat and push out into the water. Simon Peter was a pioneer and even in the context of Simon's call into the Kingdom, God asked him to take a step of faith before others. Nonetheless the Scripture paints a beautiful picture of co-laboring with Christ, for Jesus got into the boat with Simon. Our steps of faith are important both for laying vision foundations and also for casting and sharing vision with potential partners. As we respond to God's voice our steps of faith releases the manifest presence of Jesus in our midst. A wise leader understands that they can only inspire others to the extent that they themselves have modeled first fruits ministry to the Lord.

Luke 5:4, 5 Now when he had left speaking, he said unto Simon, Launch out into the deep, and let down your nets for a draught. And Simon answering said unto him, Master, we have toiled all the night, and have taken nothing: nevertheless at thy word I will let down the net.

Jesus instructed the men to let down the nets and try again even though they were tired and had spent themselves all night trying to secure a plentiful catch of fish. Nonetheless the men complied and they let out their nets one more time, trusting the Master's voice.

I have found that when we come to the end of our own strength it is then that God's grace and miracle provision are released. Trusting the

Master's voice and obeying whatever strategy He gives us will produce fruit that will last for eternity! Partnering with others in vision releases physical and spiritual resource.

Luke 5:6, 7 And when they had this done, they inclosed a great multitude of fishes: and their net brake. And they beckoned unto *their* partners, which were in the other ship, that they should come and help them. And they came, and filled both the ships, so that they began to sink.

For the fishermen, partnership and collaboration were essential in order for the maximum harvest to be brought in without loss. It was only as they worked together that the nets could be carried. Clearly if there had been only one boat on the lake, the miracle catch of fish could not have been brought to shore. As Kingdom laborers we will need anointed enterprise to bring in the full end-time harvest.

Metochos - participant i.e. (as noun) a sharer by implic. An associate – fellow, partaker, partner *"and so were James and John, the sons of Zebedee, Simon's partners (koinonos) with Simon.*

Luke 5:10 And so *was* also James, and John, the sons of Zebedee, which were partners with Simon. And Jesus said unto Simon, Fear not; from henceforth thou shalt catch men.

Koinonos – a sharer, i.e. associate – companion, x fellowship, partake, partner The Greek *Metochos* and *Koinonos* leave no doubt in our minds that the disciples shared in the Gospel ministry in companionship, fellowship and in true partnership.

They were associates together under the authority of Christ. Their commonality was found in Christ and His values and vision of the Kingdom come on earth. To represent Christ effectively, there had to be unity and agreement with the Father's heart. The same principles must co-exist today in successful Kingdom association and alliances.

Luke 5:10, 11 And so *was* also James, and John, the sons of Zebedee, which were partners with Simon. And Jesus said unto Simon, Fear not; from henceforth thou shalt catch men. And when they had brought their ships to land, they forsook all, and followed him.

These brand new disciples were required to follow Jesus with singular focus and give up everything they knew and owned in order to respond to God's call. They had to leave their comfort zone and embrace a whole new way of life. It is no different for us today. Jesus calls and compels us to the harvest fields where His presence ushers in the atmosphere of heaven and transforms the lives of the multitudes. Focus is an important quality in leaders and enables them to stay on track with vision goals. It is important to recognize that not everyone is appointed to be a primary vision carrier or pioneer leader. However, those who are primary vision carriers and who lead the way, will break new ground for those who will partner with them to become affiliates in their own field of Endeavour within the overall vision. When God called me as the primary vision carrier to lead Revival I was entrusted with the task of developing the vision, my team and partners.

• I assigned various people to appropriate departments/roles including media, administration, web design, praise coordinator, prayer etc.

• Each of the leaders of these "departments" was responsible for their particular area of expertise and was accountable to myself as the primary vision carrier.

• They in turn, became 'secondary' visionaries and vision supporters/partners within their own field of Endeavour as we fulfilled the vision together.

• My responsibility was to ensure the vision was implemented as the Lord intended and to keep an eye on the overall running of things – this did not mean I had to do all the work nor could I ever attempt to fulfill each of the areas of expertise. Partners in ministry are entrusted with assisting in this process through prayer and servant love/action.

• Each of us must seek Jesus on a personal level. It will be an ineffective association if either party is not in right relationship with Christ.

• The role of partners/supporters is to magnify Christ, lift up the hands of appointed and anointed leadership and use their own gifts and talents to help implement the vision. Team members and partners will experience personal growth and development as they are invested in by their leader(s).

• It is important that those who are not called as primary vision carriers do not assume or manipulate power or authority. Anointing does not necessarily mean one is appointed to be a leader

• A leader must be willing to serve their team and ministry partners whilst at the same time surrendering to the dominion of the Lord.

Chapter Eleven
Preparation: Commitment and Character

1

Peter 1:5, 6 Who are kept by the power of God through faith unto salvation ready to be revealed in the last time. Wherein ye greatly rejoice, though now for a season, if need be, ye are in heaviness through manifold temptations:

During the consolidation process God tests both our commitment to the vision and He also refines and tests our personal character. This testing and pruning is a necessary part of the preparation of our own foundations to carry the vision and will produce good fruit in our lives. As with natural foundations (which are usually hidden), this is a part of the preparation that very few others will see. To carry Godly vision and follow it through to completion is a costly endeavor and should not be entered into lightly. It is an act of mercy that God allows us to be refined and sharpened for His service.

God is not so interested in our competence or confidence as He is in our availability i.e. commitment is all that God requires of us. We live in a fast paced disposable society, where little value is placed on loyalty or longevity. God therefore has to ensure that we are not just in love with the notion of a vision, but that we are so in love with Him that we will follow through and finish what God has begun in us. Commitment from us will birth co-operation to the divine will of God and will produce confidence in us to co-labor with Him to fulfill vision. As a result of our co-operation with God we are made competent by grace. Our willingness to be available for God is a forerunner to divine enabling by God. God is looking for secure vessels for vision and as visionary leaders we must ensure that we let the Lord have and heal any possible areas of insecurity or wounding before stepping out to lead others in a pioneering activity. Our confidence should be in our position as legitimate sons and heirs of God. One of the most important things God taught me about vision is that carrying His presence must be my priority. To say 'yes' to the vision would mean a massive change of focus. I hadn't previously understood it from that perspective. However, after studying the life of King David my heart began to be changed by the vision. As I lived with the vision my heart was truly changed to appreciate this divine truth.

God will allow time for vision to deepen and mature in us. He permits delay and we are required to trust Him and to seek to plan within God's will. Our commitment to God and to His vision is tested in the wilderness of deferral. However, if we can learn to know our season, we can recognize its beginning and its end and we will come to understand that delay is part of the process that leads us to a new place of "promotion". By promotion I mean entering into an appointed season of being set apart and anointed as a servant leader, for Jesus teaches us that we are not to lord it over others but to have an attitude of humility just like Him. Wilderness seasons ultimately strengthen our faith and release fresh waves of adoring worship in us making us less self-reliant and more God-reliant with a singular Kingdom focus. Delay may be viewed as a developmental part of our process. One of the essential lessons I have learned during consolidation of vision and personal preparation to be a primary vision carrier is that God requires His leaders to be willing to go lower and deeper with Him, so that He can lift our vision higher. God often speaks to me in revelatory ways to teach me new Kingdom principles and to under gird known ones.

John 8:58 Jesus said unto them, Verily, verily, I say unto you, Before Abraham was, I am.

Just on the peripheral edge of my vision I turned to see Christ revealed as the Lion of the Tribe of Judah. I discerned some evil presence on the approach and Jesus had arisen to defend me. I thought of King David and how there was a God appointed time for him to go into the cave of Adullam (the stronghold of the Lord) and equally important, a God-appointed time to leave it (*1 Samuel 22:1-5*). Each season of our lives lies in the capable hands of our mighty God. Leaders are not exempt from such occurrences and it is manna to our souls to know the Master makes provision in every aspect of our journey with Him through life. At the feet of Christ, my anxious silence gave way to a state of stillness and complete peace. The darkness had passed as quickly as it had come upon me and had now completely disappeared. Lifting me to my feet once more Jesus looked at me and said, *"It's time to go deeper."*

Jesus spoke, *"**Listen**."* Intent on obeying my Master, I listened with all my heart. I clearly heard two words, *"I Am. I Am. I Am. I Am ..."* echo through time, through nations and throughout all eternity as they reached me. All that matters is who He is. He is Life itself, Breath of our breath and the DNA of all existence. "Higher, lower, deeper" in Him - the only way to go is to trust the length, breadth, depth and height of the supreme authority of God's love expressed in the words 'I Am.' The dark night of testing and trial of a child of God through isolation, rejection, ridicule and persecution can only be borne in the grace of 'I Am.' As we agree to His greatness we are overcome by His goodness and washed afresh in His blood. In wonder we listen to the echo of heaven that has resounded in the hearts of angels and mankind and we become more deeply entwined in Him. The call to "come up higher" is before the global church and her leadership. It is a holy call and the call of the Cross of our Beloved Savior. There will be both faith challenges and encounters to overcome and delight in. Each unknown step will ultimately be illuminated by the manifestation of God's glory in our lives even if the path at times seems obscured or darkened. In choosing to come up higher we must understand the passageway to this place of communion is made possible only in the humble posture of going lower.

The willingness to take up our cross is a defining lifestyle choice for every believer. When the victorious Lamb of God is lifted up in us, we are embraced, cleansed anew and enfolded in the journey of discipleship we come to know as a life of obedient faith. The Great Shepherd 'I Am' tenderly and definitely leads us to follow Him, and in trusting the path of transforming grace He has placed before each one of us, we will come to know Him more fully as 'I Am' - our strong Deliverer and mighty Provider. It is in 'going' that we become more knowing and experientially aware of the great 'I Am.' The longing to be Christ-like will cause us to cling to Him just like the woman who bled for twelve years (*Mark 5:25-34*). She clung to God in recognition that she had come to the end of herself, her resources and her strength and as she fell at Jesus' feet she experienced the reality of God's extreme Love meeting her in the place of her extreme need. Her miracle was born out of her desperation for breakthrough. are you desperate for breakthrough? Trust the Lord and throw yourself once more in mercy at His feet. He will not fail you. The devil will take us to the edge of hell, but God will deliver us safely if we will trust Him and persevere. Even as we pass through such trials God uses them to refine our faith, which is worth more than gold, to prove it genuine and result in praise, glory and honor to God.

2 Corinthians 1:4, 5 Who comforteth us in all our tribulation, that we may be able to comfort them which are in any trouble, by the comfort wherewith we ourselves are comforted of God. For as the sufferings of Christ abound in us, so our consolation also aboundeth by Christ.

"Deeper" is a costly realm of exquisite blessing, brought forth in our being found willing to identify with Christ and become more like Him. Having died with Christ to sin, we are now raised with Him in baptism of new life. (*Romans 6:4*) As we reflect on the price our Savior paid to ransom us, we become conscious of the inestimable value He has placed on each one of our souls. What love is this that flows with sacrificial mercy? It is the love of the Great 'I Am' that takes us into the depths of knowing Him and being known by Him. This word is a call to consecration - to leaders and to all believers. Jesus says, *"I Am coming back and I will return to a beautiful bride."* it is not our works that will win the world, but His work of holy passion in us that will turn the tide of wickedness and lawlessness in the nations as the floodgates of His mercy open wide.

11

⌒

Prophetic Hindrances

One thing all leaders must learn is that there are hindrances even within the gifts of the Holy Spirit. There are various stumbling blocks that will keep us from moving in the fullness of a prophetic ministry.

These include: to be tempted to use standard formulas that are outlined in various books that teach about prophetic symbolism when interpreting visions and revelations. Looking only from our personal, present perspective, we must interpret revelations not from our perspective, but from God's eternal perspective. If we interpret all revelations using the same formula, we will get inaccurate interpretations. Seeing through fear rather than faith, we're not to interpret prophecy through fear, but rather through faith. Fear is also based in suspicion and suspicion will never result in accurate interpretation. True discernment operates only in true godly love. Majoring on minors, the importance of preparing the way for the King and not primarily focusing on what the enemy is doing. Prejudices, when we prophesy we should guard against prejudice because prejudice can seriously distort a revelation and the actual meaning of it. Having prejudicial doctrines, Prophecy isn't meant to establish doctrines. That has already been established through the Bible. Rejection, Dwelling on rejection will keep us self-centered, which will distort the meaning of the revelations God is giving us as well. Bitterness, The possible result of unhealed wounds that make us sensitive in those areas. Rebellion, The refusal to submit to authority rooted in either rejection or self-will. Unsanctified mercy, having mercy about situations the Lord may be using to judge or bring correction. The important thing is to be ruled by the Holy Spirit and to gain an understanding of what God is doing. When we move in human compassion we may be tempted to take on burdens the Lord hasn't given us in the first place. The "party spirit", the temptation to believe that our ministry is the most important one and the lack of understanding that God uses all ministries to work together as one. Failing to submit to the body, God intentionally does not reveal everything to just one ministry, but reveals parts of visions and revelations to various ministries. He does that so that one ministry will depend on others, and a working together to understand the entire picture is essential. Lust, "One of the primary destroyers of prophetic vision." We need to put a guard on our eyes so our eyes are single and thereby the entire body can be full of God's light. In this way we won't use our eyes for evil. Using natural eyes instead of the "eye of our heart", We must understand that the things of God must be interpreted by the Spirit and not by our own perspectives and reasoning. Our words speak either life or death. As we grow in the prophetic and in our relationship with God we will find more and more that there is power in our words especially when God puts His anointing on them. A word spoken within the right timing and God's anointing is very powerful. It is important that we abide in the Word itself for God uses His Word to express Himself in His language. We learn the spiritual (symbolic) language through dreams and visions. Like many things, it requires time and patience to produce lasting fruit. A problem won't be eliminated by dealing with the symptoms. Instead we must put the ax to the root of the problem tree - deal with the source and thereby also remove the symptoms. The Lord works a deep work from the inside out, not the outside in. It's that type of working that will create deep and lasting changes. God is a practical God and His fruit is a practical fruit. It needs to be our goal to not just bear fruit, but to bear fruit that lasts. It requires patience to bear lasting fruit. But it's worth the wait because when there is lasting fruit, Christ will be lifted up by His people and "all men will be drawn to Him."

Removing Hindrances

Prophecy is conditional and we have to cooperate with God to bring the Word to pass. The biggest thing that you must understand is that there are many hindrances to prophecy. There are many spiritual and personal hindrances that are meant to block you from the fulfillment of prophecies. The first one I want to talk about is inpatients. We always want it now. Personal prophecy is not going to come to pass in our time but God's. Do you want to be in a desert like Moses for forty years? Every time we fail to wait patiently until God reveals His divine way. We have to wait until God's appointed time for prophecy is fulfilled. God knows all the things that must happen before our prophecies can come to pass. We are to take it one step at a time. I also have seen many people that always have someone to blame for a problem. If we get mad and blame someone for a problem it can cause us to get mad at God and everyone else. This in turn can cause the final result in not receiving the promise of the Lord. Many Christians seem to keep a mindset that will hinder prophecy. Preconceived ideas will not allow personal prophecies to change our way of thinking. People reject a prophecy just because of a mindset.

Look at this,

Matthew 18:21-22 Then came Peter to him, and said, Lord, how oft shall my brother sin against me, and I forgive him? till seven times? Jesus saith unto him, I say not unto thee, Until seven times: but, Until seventy times seven.

Even when Jesus talked to the disciples about the death and resurrection they rejected it. It didn't line up with their thinking. In the Litchfield Revival God spoke that it would end and they didn't receive it. It went against their mindset. If it was up to Jesus' disciples He would have never went to the cross. How many of us are stuck in a mindset about something in our lives. I have seen the most powerful self-hindrance is pride. It is the most dangerous of fulfillment of personal prophecy. Pride if we let it will do more than just hinder personal prophecy but it can destroy our ministry from ever coming into its fullness. Unbelief is always there trying to convince us that what we may know to be true is false. Unbelief means that you once believed and now don't believe. If you ever feel like you have been in a desert place for a long time you may be dealing with unbelief. I know for me I have dealt with procrastination when it comes to fulfilling personal prophecies. Putting off what God has told us to do can get us in trouble. We need to act on what we can do so God will do what we cannot do.

If we deal with a poor self-image it can alter our personal prophecies. If we have a complex we can really mishandle the Words from God. God will have a harder time convincing someone of something that has a poor self-image. When people are trying for years to make something happen, but nothing happens. The soul will try to defend itself by rejecting prophecy. We don't want to be disappointed again and we reject the prophecy. If you get a defeated spirit it hinders prophecy. Remember we need to guard our heart, mind and emotions. God is faithful to watch over His Word to perform it. When you receive a personal prophecy it most likely will seem impossible. We need to focus on the promise rather than the evidence and we will step into God's opportunity. God loves to see us through the impossibilities. If we want personal prophecy to come to pass we must respond properly. I want to deal with the hindrance of improper response. We limit the power and prophetic promise by an improper response to the Word. If a prophetic person tells us something that we are to do, we should do it. Obedience is the only way to fulfill God's promise.

Matthew 13:3-13 And he spake many things unto them in parables, saying, Behold, a sower went forth to sow; And when he sowed, some *seeds* fell by the way side, and the fowls came and devoured them up: Some fell upon stony places, where they had not much earth: and forthwith they sprung up, because they had no deepness of earth: And when the sun was up, they were scorched; and because they had no root, they withered away. And some fell among thorns; and the thorns sprung up, and choked them: But other fell into good ground, and brought forth fruit, some an hundredfold, some sixtyfold, some thirtyfold. Who hath ears to hear, let him hear. And the disciples came, and said unto him, Why speakest thou unto them in parables? He answered and said unto them, Because it is given unto you to know the mysteries of the kingdom of heaven, but to them it is not given. For whosoever hath, to him shall be given, and he shall have more abundance: but whosoever hath not, from him shall be taken away even that he hath. Therefore speak I to them in parables: because they seeing see not; and hearing they hear not, neither do they understand.

We can have such improper responses to the Word by the ability to retain the Word that can cause us to a weak response. This is the heart of the selfish people pleaser. Another improper response is worldly (a life of sin) and it causes personal prophecies to be chocked out and kills God's plans for a person. You can receive prophecy and be in the world (living in sin) but it doesn't mean God will force His will on anyone. Another hindrance is misinterpretation and manipulation of prophecy. We can hear from God and how we apply the Word can hinder it from coming to pass. We can take prophecy to lightly by not following it seriously. Personal prophecy is nothing to play with. You cannot manipulate the Word. I've seen people try to personally cause prophecies to come to pass. God accepts no substitute for obedience, regardless of how beneficial it may seem. Sometimes the blockage is in the soul of a man. This consists of emotion, desire or ambition. We can let our emotions hinder God's Words from the fulfillment and fear man instead of God.

Jeremiah 38:19 And Zedekiah the king said unto Jeremiah, I am afraid of the Jews that are fallen to the Chaldeans, lest they deliver me into their hand, and they mock me.

1 Samuel 15:24 And Saul said unto Samuel, I have sinned: for I have transgressed the commandment of the LORD, and thy words: because I feared the people, and obeyed their voice.

Our feelings can prevent us from faith for the Word when we have a personal dislike for the person giving the Word or the prophecy. When things don't work out the way we want disappointment can hinder fulfillment of God's Word. If you have had disappointments it can cause you to expect to be disappointed. It can cause a lack of faith for the Word. We must be willing to wait despite apparent failure of the prophecy and willing to go through God's process. There are many spiritual hindrances where prophecies are concerned. You can read about them all in the "Defeating the Demonic Realm"

12

⌇

Removing Torment of Ministry

There is a certain torment that ministry can bring. Most people don't understand that but once you have spent a year in the ministry, you will learn there are irritations that will arise. Unfortunately, we live in an age and in a society where the image we have of our local minister (or evangelist or teacher) is that of someone who is high on a pedestal, three miles removed from the anguish of the tormenting fears of Satan. The minister then feels a tremendous inner burden to live up to his stainless steel image. Tremendous energy drains out of his innermost being as he struggles day after day to "keep the mask on." Publicly, he usually succeeds.

But the turmoil raging inside his soul is another matter. There, he carries on more wars with fear and anxiety than most of us could ever deal with. When God leads us to pray for the sick or to work miracles, we are beginning to take courage to do it. In many cases, while we are beginning to pray or move on it, fear hits us, and we are not able to complete the work.

Oh, how the fear of man is keeping hundreds of thousands of people and their pastors not only away from the blessings of God, but away from obeying Jesus and moving out in the power of God! Pastors are afraid of their congregations. Congregations are afraid of their pastors. Pastors are afraid of each other, afraid that the church down the street might get a few more tithe-paying sheep. I can just hear the agonizing cry of our Lord as He warns and pleads with us:

Luke 12:4, 5 And I say unto you my friends, Be not afraid of them that kill the body, and after that have no more that they can do. But I will forewarn you whom ye shall fear: Fear him, which after he hath killed hath power to cast into hell; yea, I say unto you, Fear him.

Right now, God is looking for thousands of pastors, ministers, and evangelists like this man. Before Christ returns, He is going to purge His Body of all of the dead works that we've been locked into because of fear, all of the cold, joyless formalism which holds congregations in bondage because their pastors are afraid of the Spirit of God.

How my heart grieves to see so many of you, who long to sing, to testify, and to move out in the gifts of the Holy Spirit, hold back because you're afraid you will say the wrong thing. You hold words of life "in your hands," and are afraid to deliver them! There are whole congregations who are terrified to lift up their hands to the Lord or to issue a prayer request at a small gathering. Of course, giving a prophecy or a message in tongues is out of the question!

So many people long to see the gifts of the Holy Spirit in operation (the gifts that God gave to us to build and equip His Church), but the pastors are so afraid of their people "getting in the flesh" that they never get in the Spirit.

One man started to get the Baptism of the Holy Ghost in my meeting. He began to speak in other tongues. Then, all of a sudden, he stopped. I asked him, "Why did you stop after you started to speak?" He answered, "When I started speaking, it sounded like I myself was speaking. I got to thinking that it was me and not God, and I became afraid."

You do not have to be afraid. God, your Father, will not give you something that isn't of Him (see Luke 11:11,13). Do not be afraid to "let go." The Word of God commands us:

Romans 12:11 Not slothful in business; fervent in spirit; serving the Lord;

God literally dwells in the praises of His people (see Psalms 22:3). You need never be afraid to use all of the talents that He Himself has put within you to enable you to worship Him in spirit and in truth. You do not have to fear anybody else's opinion when He gives you a Word which will heal or encourage one of His suffering lambs. You need only to stand up and give it! If you insist on living in the fear of being emotional or of being "in the flesh," you will never know what it is like to be used of God in the Spirit.

Acts 1:8 But ye shall receive power, after that the Holy Ghost is come upon you: and ye shall be witnesses unto me both in Jerusalem, and in all Judaea, and in Samaria, and unto the uttermost part of the earth.

Satan is keeping many of you so bound by fear that you can't even witness to your neighbor or fellow worker at your job.

The strongest satanic deception in the Church today is that Satan's demons operate only outside the Body of Christ, and that when it comes to Christians, these demons have no real power. Meanwhile, the demonic spirit of fear is keeping a majority of God's people tied up in fruitless bondage, deceived into thinking that it's all right to sit back and wait for heaven—when, in reality, they are headed for "outer darkness."

All of this directly relates to Satan's second most destructive deception.

One of the most destructive deceptions from Satan is that your fear affects you alone. There are literally thousands of different fears that bind the Church today. Every day we face the fear of cats, trees, cars, airplanes, being alone, being rejected, being around people, intimacy, relationships, responsibility, commitment, poverty, success, losing what you have, the opinions of others, and impending sicknesses. But the one deception that Satan has succeeded in pulling off in the minds of all of those who fear, is that failure to overcome your little fear is no big deal because it affects you and you alone.

Let me tell you something. No fear that you hang onto or fail to get the victory over ever affects only you alone! We are all one in the Spirit, and any fear which hinders you ultimately has a devastating effect on the whole Body of Christ in the spirit world.

This is why God has always refused to allow the fearful to remain in His Army! In essence He told them: Go home. We don't want you. We don't need you. When we go to war you'll only contaminate the others. (See Deuteronomy 20:8 and Judges 7:3.)

In God's Army today it doesn't matter what your fear is. The truth is that all fear originates from a demonic spirit of fear who has gained a foothold in your mind and is an archenemy of God. If this spirit of fear is allowed to retain its foothold, sooner or later it will rise up to hinder, block, and prevent Christ's life from flowing through you when you need it the most.

Are you ready to do something about it?

In many ways God's army today is like the children of Israel were when they came out of Egypt. After they were delivered, what was the first thing they were faced with? The Red Sea! What was their reaction to it? They were paralyzed with fear! Fear literally overtook their minds as they turned against Moses, complaining:

Exodus 14:11 And they said unto Moses, Because *there were* no graves in Egypt, hast thou taken us away to die in the wilderness? wherefore hast thou dealt thus with us, to carry us forth out of Egypt?

At first, Moses desperately tried to encourage them by telling them to hang in there. "Just stand still," he said. "The Lord will fight for you." But at that point the Lord Himself broke in with a direct command: *"Quit praying and get the people moving! Forward, march!"* (Exodus 14:15 TLB).

These are the same orders our Commander is giving us now. He is telling us that it's time to quit whining about our fears and time to get moving in our offensive warfare against the devil. Therefore, as of today, you and I are going to go after every demonic power of fear that is binding your life and destroying your witness for Christ!

We are going to rip the mask right off of the devil and his tactics, openly and without fear.

I have exposed his strategies and am providing you with a foundation for conquering him in every aspect of your life. You are not going to hide.

You are not going to remain on the defensive. You are not fighting a war of preservation.

God's Word has already told us why He sent His Son to deliver us. It was:

Luke 1:74, 75 That he would grant unto us, that we being delivered out of the hand of our enemies might serve him without fear, In holiness and righteousness before him, all the days of our life.

Bless God, you have heard His battle cry against fear in your heart. You are now going to come down out of your high tower of intellectual knowledge and move out onto the battlefield. All of the joy, courage, confidence, peace, vitality, and zeal that Satan has stolen from you through fear will be restored to you in the mighty Name of Jesus.

2 Timothy 1:7 For God hath not given us the spirit of fear; but of power, and of love, and of a sound mind.

Get ready. You are about to begin a victorious life!

13

~

Foundations of Religion

First of all you must realize that Religion is not at all what God intended. He wants a relationship with us. Guilt is a major part of this foundation.

Eli, the priest who raised the prophet Samuel, is a biblical example of someone who ministered in a religious spirit founded upon guilt. Eli had so much zeal for the Lord that when he heard the Ark had been captured by the Philistines, he fell over and died. He had spent his life trying to serve the Lord as a high priest, but the very first prophetic word given to Samuel was one of the most frightening rebukes given in the Scriptures—and it was directed to Eli!

1 Samuel 3:13, 14 For I have told him that I will judge his house for ever for the iniquity which he knoweth; because his sons made themselves vile, and he restrained them not. And therefore I have sworn unto the house of Eli, that the iniquity of Eli's house shall not be purged with sacrifice nor offering for ever.

Eli's zeal for the Lord was based on sacrifices and offerings intended to compensate for his irresponsibility as a father. Guilt can spur us on to great zeal for the Lord and our sacrifices and offerings become an attempt to atone for our failures. We should note here that the Lord never said that Eli's sin couldn't be forgiven. He said that Eli's attempts to atone for sin *by sacrifice and offering* would never succeed. There are multitudes of men and women whose zeal for the Lord is likewise based on an attempt to atone for sin, failure, or irresponsibility in other areas of their lives. But all the sacrifices in the world will not atone for even our smallest failure. To even make such an attempt is an insult to the cross of Jesus, which is the only acceptable sacrifice to the Father for sin.

Attempting to gain God's approval by our own sacrifice opens the door wide for a religious spirit, because such service is not based on the blood of Jesus, but on an attempt to make our own compensation for sin. This does not mean we should not do things to please the Lord; it means our motive for pleasing the Lord is for His joy, not for our acceptance. One is God-centered; the other is self-centered. And this is self-centeredness of the most destructive kind—an attempt to avoid the cross.

It is also noteworthy that one of the sins of Eli's sons was that they "...despised the offering of the Lord" (1 Sam. 2:17).

They appropriated for their own selfish use the sacrifices and offerings brought to the Lord. Those who are gripped by this form of a religious spirit will often be the most zealous to preach the cross, but herein lies the perversion: It emphasizes *their* cross more than the cross of Jesus. Their real delight is more in self-abasement than in the cross of Christ, which alone makes us righteous and acceptable to God.

Idealism is one of the most deceptive and destructive disguises of the religious spirit. Idealism is of human origin and is a form of humanism. Although it has the appearance of seeking only the highest standards and the preservation of God's glory, idealism is possibly the most deadly enemy of true revelation and true grace. It is deadly because it does not allow for growing up into grace and wisdom, rather it attacks and destroys the foundation of those who are in pursuit of God's glory, but are not yet there.

Idealism imposes on others standards that are beyond what God has required or given the grace for at that time. For example, men controlled by this kind of religious spirit may condemn those who are not praying two hours a day as they are. The truth is, it may be God's will for us to be praying that much, but how we get there is crucial. The grace of God may first call us to pray just ten minutes a day. Then, as we become so blessed by His presence, we will not want to quit after ten minutes but instead spend more and more time with Him until we pray for an hour, then two. When we are eventually praying two hours a day, it will be because of our love for prayer and the presence of the Lord, not out of fear or pride.

A person with a religious spirit based on idealism will usually seek the perfect church, and will refuse to be a part of anything less. Those led by the Holy Spirit may also have high hopes for a church, but will still be able to give themselves in service to even some of the most lowly works, in order to help those works grow in vision and maturity. The Holy Spirit is called "the Helper" (John 14:26), and those who are truly led by the Spirit will always be looking for ways to help, not to stand aloof and criticize.

When a religious spirit is founded upon pride, it is evidenced by *perfectionism*. The perfectionist sees everything as black or white. This develops into extremes, requiring that every person and every teaching be judged as either 100 percent right or 100 percent wrong. This is a standard with which only Jesus could comply. It will lead to a serious delusion when we impose it on ourselves or others. True grace imparts a truth that sets people free, showing them the way out of their sin, and beckoning them to higher levels of spiritual maturity.

One with a religious spirit can usually point to problems with great accuracy, but seldom has solutions, except to tear down what has already been built. This is the strategy of the enemy to nullify progress that is being made and to sow discouragement that will limit future progress. This produces the mentality that if we cannot go straight to the top of the mountain, we should not climb at all, but just "die to self." This is a death that God has not required and it is a perversion of the exhortation for us to take up our crosses daily.

The perfectionist both imposes and tries to live by standards that stifle true maturity and growth. The grace of God will lead us up the mountain step-by-step. The Lord does not condemn us because we may trip a few times while trying to climb. He graciously picks us up with the encouragement that we can make it. We must have a vision of making it to the top, and should never condemn ourselves for not being there yet, *as long as we are still climbing*.

James said, "...we all stumble in many ways..." (James. 3:2).

If we had to wait until we were perfect before we could minister, no one would ever qualify for the ministry. Even though perfect obedience and understanding should always be our goal, such will never be found within ourselves, but only as we come to perfectly abide in the Perfect One.

Because "now we see through a glass, darkly" (1 Corinthians 13:12 KJV), or in part, we must always be open to greater accuracy in our beliefs and teachings. One of the greatest delusions of all is that we are already complete in our understanding, or 100 percent accurate in our perceptions or actions. Those with a religious spirit will usually claim to be open to more understanding, but most of the time this is done to convince *everyone else* to be open to what they teach, while they remain steadfastly closed to others.

Jesus blessed Peter and turned the keys of the kingdom over to him just before He had to rebuke him by calling him "satan".

Matthew 16:23 But he turned, and said unto Peter, Get thee behind me, Satan: thou art an offence unto me: for thou savourest not the things that be of God, but those that be of men.

Right after this greatest of blessings, the enemy deceived him, yet the Lord did not take the keys away from Peter! In fact, Jesus knew when He gave the keys to Peter that he would soon deny even knowing Him.

Many years after Peter used the keys to open the door of faith for both the Jews and Gentiles, "the least of the apostles," Paul, had to rebuke him publicly because of his hypocrisy (see 1 Corinthians 15:9, Galatians 2:11-14). Even so, Peter was promised that he would sit on one of the twelve thrones judging the twelve tribes of Israel (see Matthew 19:28). The Lord has proven that He will commission and use men long before most of us would, and when He calls us, He already knows all the mistakes that we will make.

It seems that the Lord's leadership style was to provide a place where

His followers could make mistakes and learn from them. We must correct mistakes, because that is how we learn, but it must be a correction that encourages and frees, not one that condemns and crushes initiative.

One of the most powerful and deceptive forms of the religious spirit is built upon the foundations of both fear and pride. Those who are bound in this way go through periods of deep anguish and remorse at their failures, but this false repentance results only in more self-abasement and further attempts to make sacrifices that will appease the Lord. Those bound by this religious spirit then often flip to the other side, where they become so convinced that they are superior to other Christians or other groups that they become unteachable and unable to receive reproof. The foundation that they stand on at any given time will be dictated more by external pressure than by true conviction. Such a religious spirit is so slippery that it will wiggle out of almost any attempt to confront it. If you address the pride, the fears and insecurities will rise up to attract sympathy. If you confront the fear, it will then change into religious pride masquerading as faith. This type of spirit will drive individuals or congregations to such extremes that they will inevitably disintegrate.

A religious spirit will usually give a counterfeit gift of discernment of spirits that is motivated by suspicion and fear. This counterfeit gift thrives on seeing what is wrong with others rather than seeing what God is doing so we can help them along. Using this type of discernment, a religious spirit can cause some of its greatest damage to the Church. Its ministry will almost always leave more damage and division than healing, reconciliation, and building. Its wisdom is rooted in the Tree of the Knowledge of Good and Evil, and though the truth may be accurate, it is ministered in a spirit that kills.

Suspicion is rooted in such things as rejection, territorial preservation, or general insecurity. The true gift of discernment can only function through love.

Any motive other than love will distort spiritual perception. Whenever someone submits a judgment or criticism about another person or group, we should disregard it unless we know that the one bringing it truly loves that person or group, and has an "investment" of service to them.

As you have probably already assumed, all evil spiritual strongholds have similar characteristics. Their tactics and functions often overlap to become a web that captures and then holds its prey. Of all the fortresses of deception that the enemy has built among men, the religious spirit has been the most deceptive and deadly, because it comes as a pretense of righteousness and goodness.

Even though this spirit comes with a pretense for righteousness, it is discerned by how it always has us looking at ourselves, trying to measure ourselves against standards, comparing ourselves to others, and consequently distracting us from the glory of God that transforms us. The religious spirit is therefore the most concentrated fruit from the Tree of the Knowledge of Good and Evil. The "good" side of this tree is just as deadly as the evil—the fruit of the religious spirit will always be spiritual death.

14

⌒

The Purpose of Prophetic

If you are to have a successful Church or ministry, there must be prophetic. The prophetic is necessary for where we are going. There are people beginning to walk in realms of super-natural encounters and divine revelation, "What is the purpose of the prophetic gifting?" Why does God give revelatory graces to His children? The answer is simple to state, but pro-found in its working out in our lives: God gives revelatory graces to His children to reveal in us, and to a desperate and needy world, the glorious Person of His Son, Jesus Christ. That revelation has life-changing power, not only for non-believers brought to faith because of it, but also for believers whose faith walk and ministry is forever transformed by a personal, God encounter.

Having said that, I want to consider supplemental purposes for God's revelatory graces—along with some scriptural examples—that serve the ultimate purpose of drawing us closer to Him.

Dreams and visions are used to reveal God's promises.

In Genesis 28:10-15, we find the account of "Jacob's ladder." Fleeing home for fear of his brother Esau's wrath, Jacob stops at a particular location in the wilderness for the night. Using a rock for a pillow, Jacob falls asleep and dreams of a ladder that links Heaven and earth and has God's angels ascending and descending its steps. Atop the ladder, Jacob saw the Lord, who gave him a wonderful promise:

Genesis 28:13-15 And, behold, the LORD stood above it, and said, I *am* the LORD God of Abraham thy father, and the God of Isaac: the land whereon thou liest, to thee will I give it, and to thy seed; And thy seed shall be as the dust of the earth, and thou shalt spread abroad to the west, and to the east, and to the north, and to the south: and in thee and in thy seed shall all the families of the earth be blessed. And, behold, I *am* with thee, and will keep thee in all *places* whither thou goest, and will bring thee again into this land; for I will not leave thee, until I have done *that* which I have spoken to thee of.

God's promise to Jacob was a reaffirmation of the promise given to both Abraham and Isaac, who were Jacob's grandfather and father, respectively: Their descendants would become a great nation and would inherit and occupy the land of Canaan.

This dream had an immediate, profound impact on Jacob. upon awakening, Jacob was filled with awe and fear, and said, "Surely the Lord is in this place, and I did not know it...How awesome is this place! This is none other than the house of God, and this is the gate of heaven" (Genesis 28:16-17). Taking the stone he had used for a pillow, Jacob established a memorial to his God encounter; then he anointed it with oil and worshiped the Lord. Jacob vowed that if God would protect and provide for him, then he would serve the Lord. Jacob's transformation was not completed overnight, but that one dream sent him well on his way to being changed from Jacob (whose name means "deceiver") to Israel (whose name means "prince of God").

Supernatural encounters often give direction, especially at major turning points.

Consider Joseph's dilemma in the first chapter of Matthew. Betrothed to Mary, Joseph learns that she is pregnant and, not wishing to disgrace her publicly, plans to divorce her quietly. That is, until an angel visits Joseph in a dream and gives counsel that changes both his mind and course of action: "Joseph, son of David, do not be afraid to take Mary as your wife; for the Child who has been conceived in her is of the Holy Spirit. She will bear a Son; and you shall call His name Jesus, for He will save His people from their sins" (Matthew 1:20b-21). Joseph's revelatory experience gave him direction to help him make the right decision.

In Acts 16:9, the apostle Paul receives a vision in which a man appeals for him to come to Macedonia. This experience leads to the first evangelistic thrust into Europe. Prior to Paul's vision, he and his companions had tried to take the gospel into both Asia and Bithynia, but each time the Holy Spirit forbade them from doing so. Only Paul's Macedonian vision gave them direction to know where to go.

Revelatory experiences give warnings.

In Matthew 2:12, a dream warns the wise men not to report back to King Herod, so they end up returning home by a different route. In the very next verse, an angel warns Joseph to take Mary and Jesus and flee to Egypt to escape Herod's murderous rage. Sometime after Herod's death, Joseph is told in another dream that it is now safe to return home.

In Acts 22:17-21, Paul relates how—while praying in Jerusalem—he fell into a trance and a vision of the Lord warned him to flee because the Jews would not accept Paul's testimony about Him. In God's plan for His people, there is a time to stand and a time to flee. In this instance, the time was for Paul to flee. As Paul indicates in verse 21, this warning from the Lord first propelled him into carrying the gospel to the Gentiles.

Dreams and visions give instruction.

Job 33:14-18 For God speaketh once, yea twice, *yet man* perceiveth it not. In a dream, in a vision of the night, when deep sleep falleth upon men, in slumberings upon the bed; Then he openeth the ears of men, and sealeth their instruction, That he may withdraw man *from his* purpose, and hide pride from man. He keepeth back his soul from the pit, and his life from perishing by the sword.

God speaks once, twice, and numerous times, and in a variety of different ways—including dreams and visions—so as to open men's ears and seal His instruction. The Lord's gracious and redemptive purpose is to turn men from their evil ways and prevent them from going to hell by leading them into knowledge of righteousness.

For years, Christians around the world have been praying for God to visit the Muslim people. As a general rule, Muslims hold a strong belief in the power of dreams. Not long ago, an international leader of Youth with a Mission reported that in Algeria (a primarily Muslim nation) some 10,000 Muslims had the same dream on the same night: Jesus appeared in all these dreams. As a result of this supernatural encounter, these Muslims came to faith in Christ.

Sometimes God gives dreams and visions to turn people from darkness and error to truth and light. His purpose is to deliver their souls from hell because, as Ezekiel 33:11 says, God takes "no pleasure in the death of the wicked, but rather that the wicked turn from his way and live" and He "desires all men to be saved and to come to the knowledge of the truth" (1 Timothy 2:4). Part of God's last days great purposes is to release conviction in the human spirit through revelatory graces.

In the Spirit of revelation, God can deal with a man in a special way.

The prophetic has a way of cutting through our traditions and hard outside "crust" to pierce our spirit. No matter what our tradition, theology, or doctrinal background, when God wants to get our attention, He can do it through prophetic expression. God dealt with King Solomon in a particular way through a dream. First Kings 3:5 says: "In Gibeon the Lord appeared to Solomon in a dream at night; and God said, 'Ask what you wish Me to give you.' " If God came to you with such an open-ended offer, what would you ask for? Out of all the possibilities Solomon could have chosen, he asked for wisdom to rule his people well. God was so pleased with Solomon's selfless request that He gave him not only wisdom, but riches and honor greater than any who came before or after him.

I believe that it is significant that God used a dream to communicate with Solomon in this instance. Notice that the verse says that "the Lord appeared to Solomon." Was this a pre-incarnate appearance of Christ, the second Person of the Godhead? No one knows. At the very least, Solomon understood from his dream that he was being spoken to by God and not just an angelic being.

Prophetic activity predicts the future.

The Bible contains many examples of the prophetic predicting future events. For instance, in Daniel 2, the King of Babylon dreams about future kingdoms to arise after the Babylonian empire is no more. Neither the king, nor any of his wise men, could understand the dream, but Daniel does an interpretation as the Spirit of God gives him understanding. The Babylonian kingdom will be followed by empires built by the MedoPersian, Greek, and Roman peoples. After these empires of men collapse, a divine Kingdom will come that will last forever.

The Book of Luke speaks of Zacharias, a priest who has a vision of an angel while he ministers in the temple. The angel tells Zacharias that he and his wife Elisabeth, who is barren, will have a son to be named John. Nine months later, Elisabeth does bear a son, who grows up to be known as John the Baptist and who, according to Jesus, is the greatest prophet to have ever walked the earth.

Prophetic gifts give courage.

Paul was ministering in Corinth after having suffered hardship and persecution for the sake of the gospel in city after city. What lay ahead for him in Corinth? Paul was no different from us; in his lowest moments, he must have wondered at times whether all his hard work and sacrifice truly made any difference. In Paul's hour of need, the Lord brought him encouragement:

Acts 18:9, 10 Then spake the Lord to Paul in the night by a vision, Be not afraid, but speak, and hold not thy peace: For I am with thee, and no man shall set on thee to hurt thee: for I have much people in this city.

Month after month and place after place, Paul had labored hard and faithfully, often alone and against fierce opposition and hostility. How reassuring it must have been to hear that, in Corinth, the Lord had "many people." With these like-minded believers, Paul could work, worship, and fellowship. Instead of being run out of town for preaching the gospel, as had happened so often, Paul could settle down for a year-and-a-half of teaching God's word free from persecution. This period of rest and respite renewed Paul's strength and gave him courage to continue the Lord's work.

Years later, Paul was sailing to Rome as an imperial prisoner to be tried before the emperor. A violent, two-week-long storm at sea caught up Paul, his traveling companions, the ship's crew, and a contingent of Roman soldiers guarding all the prisoners. Just when everyone else had almost given up hope, Paul spoke to the entire company:

Acts 27:22-26 And now I exhort you to be of good cheer: for there shall be no loss of *any man's* life among you, but of the ship. For there stood by me this night the angel of God, whose I am, and whom I serve, Saying, Fear not, Paul; thou must be brought before Caesar: and, lo, God hath given thee all them that sail with thee. Wherefore, sirs, be of good cheer: for I believe God, that it shall be even as it was told me. Howbeit we must be cast upon a certain island.

The account says that Paul's words encouraged all on board and restored their hope. In the end, events transpired in precisely the manner foretold to Paul by the angel. The ship ran aground and was battered to pieces by the waves, but everyone aboard made it safely to shore. As it happened, they had arrived on the island of Malta, where they spent three winter months.

Dreams and visions are a major way that God communicates to His prophets.

In Numbers 12:6, God says: "Hear now My words: If there is a prophet among you, I, the Lord, shall make Myself known to him in a vision. I shall speak with him in a dream." There's not much else to be said: For prophets and other prophetic people, dreams and visions come with the territory.

Revelatory graces draw us into worship.

Do you remember the story of Gideon? God raised up Gideon as a judge to deliver the Israelites from continuous attack from the Midianites. Gideon put out his fleece to verify that God had spoken, then went out and amassed an army of 32,000, which the Lord pared down to 300 men. Then, with their trumpets, torches, and clay pitchers, Gideon and his men surrounded the Midianite camp. The night before the battle, Gideon needed a little extra encouragement, so the Lord directs him to sneak into the enemy's camp. While there, he overhears two Midianites talking.

Judges 7:13-15 And when Gideon was come, behold, *there was* a man that told a dream unto his fellow, and said, Behold, I dreamed a dream, and, lo, a cake of barley bread tumbled into the host of Midian, and came unto a tent, and smote it that it fell, and overturned it, that the tent lay along. And his fellow answered and said, This *is* nothing else save the sword of Gideon the son of Joash, a man of Israel: *for* into his hand hath God delivered Midian, and all the host. And it was *so,* when Gideon heard the telling of the dream, and the interpretation thereof, that he worshipped, and returned into the host of Israel, and said, Arise; for the LORD hath delivered into your hand the host of Midian.

Hearing God's plan come from the mouth of a pagan Midianite was all the confirmation Gideon needed. He returned to his own camp absolutely convinced and confident of victory. Notice what Gideon did before returning to camp, however: He bowed in worship. In humility and devotion Gideon acknowledged God as the Source of the revelation and the victory that was sure to come. Gideon's revelatory experience served several purposes. First, it revealed a promise—that God had delivered the Midianites into Gideon's hands. Second, it predicted the future—victory for Gideon and his men. Third, it gave Gideon courage to follow through with God's command. Fourth, it inspired Gideon to worship the Lord. That should be the effect of all revelatory graces upon our lives—they should draw us into worship. When-ever God speaks, He always does so in an incredibly personal fashion. He speaks to us out of symbols of the past; He knows our strengths, our weaknesses, and our failures; and He knows our destination. In the midst of it all, He comes to strengthen us with His power, enlighten us with His revelation, and encourage us with reminders of our destiny. Our response should be one of praise, humble surrender, and joyous worship.

Prophetic encounters cast new light and grant new perspective.

God's prophetic revelatory graces can enlighten us to past events, our current understanding, and even future incidents. Remember when Elisha and his servant were surrounded by the Syrians. Once God opened the servant's eyes to see the flaming chariots and their angelic occupants, his entire perspective on the situation changed. The revelatory grace God bestowed on him—as a result of Elisha's prayer—cast a whole new light on his circumstances.

Here's another example: In Chapter 8, we discussed healing dreams as one category of self-disclosure dreams. In a healing dream, the Lord can pull something negative or hurtful out of our past and—by casting a new light or granting new perspective—give us a redemptive reinterpretation so that it is no longer a source of pain.

As with anything profitable in the Spirit, there are traps to avoid when getting into revelatory giftings.

1. Don't forget the basic spiritual disciplines. The revelatory word is meant to complement the Word of God, *not* compete with it. We need to be addicted to God and His Word, not to personal prophecy.

2. Don't forget the Body of Christ. Christianity is a relational faith; there is no place for "lone rangers." Don't let yourself become puffed up with arrogance because of your many revelations. Be a practical, functioning member of the Body of Christ in your given locality. Seek godly counsel and a network of caring people. Avoid becoming a prophet in isolation.

   Four traits in particular are especially dangerous for prophetic people: alienation; isolation; rejection; and pride. The danger of developing any of these qualities is part of the risk of walking in prophetic territory, so be careful to guard against them.

3. Watch out for revelation fixation. Don't get so caught up in any particular aspect of your revelatory experience that you stop looking or listening before receiving the full message.

Daniel 7 records an awesome, terrifying vision in which each image is more captivating than the previous one. Throughout the chapter, Daniel repeatedly "kept on looking." He didn't become fixated on any particular image, no matter how thrilling or terrifying it was. Instead, he pressed on and watched closely for the vision's endpoint so that he could receive its full understanding.

The first part of Daniel's vision focused on the prevalence of wickedness and evil on the earth. Had Daniel stopped looking at that point, he would have had a "revelation" of continuing evil and despair.

At the end of the vision, however, Daniel sees the prophetic promise of God's triumphant Kingdom—one that destroys and supplants all evil empires of mankind and brings His rule upon the earth. That is an entirely different revelation, and one Daniel would have missed had he stopped looking too soon.

Do not become fixated upon revelation of evil. Do not be impressed with the devil's plans; only be impressed with God's revival plan, as revealed in Jeremiah 29:11-14:

Jeremiah 29:11-14 For I know the thoughts that I think toward you, saith the LORD, thoughts of peace, and not of evil, to give you an expected end. Then shall ye call upon me, and ye shall go and pray unto me, and I will hearken unto you. And ye shall seek me, and find *me,* when ye shall search for me with all your heart. And I will be found of you, saith the LORD: and I will turn away your captivity, and I will gather you from all the nations, and from all the places whither I have driven you, saith the LORD; and I will bring you again into the place whence I caused you to be carried away captive.

The reality of evil is part of the picture, but not its entirety. Be like Daniel and press ahead for the whole picture; keep looking, asking, and pressing in until filled with revelation of who this Son of God is and His purposes in the earth. Chapter 5 of Amos charges us to: "Seek the Lord that you may live...Seek good and not evil, that you may live; and thus may the Lord God of hosts be with you" (Amos 5:6b, 14a). We need to keep looking until we see the Lord Himself. He wants to reveal more than just His plans and His ways: He wants to reveal Himself.

According to Malachi 4:5, prophets and other prophetic people are forerunners: "Behold, I am going to send you Elijah the prophet before the coming of the great and the terrible day of the Lord." In other words, God's revelatory graces are given to help prepare the way for fulfillment of His plans and promises. The Gospels of Luke and Matthew both plainly identify John the Baptist as the prophetic fulfillment of Malachi 4:5. John the Baptist was the "Elijah" who came as a forerunner to prepare the way for Christ's birth. He was the first true prophet to the Jews in over 400 years, and the last of the Old Testament-style prophets. Simeon and Anna, who figure prominently in Luke's account of the nativity, were also prophetic vessels whose words helped usher the way for the Child. People with prophetic graces also help prepare the way for Christ's second coming.

Acts 3:19-21 Repent ye therefore, and be converted, that your sins may be blotted out, when the times of refreshing shall come from the presence of the Lord; And he shall send Jesus Christ, which before was preached unto you: Whom the heaven must receive until the times of restitution of all things, which God hath spoken by the mouth of all his holy prophets since the world began.

Proper revelation is needed to bring about biblical restoration. The second and third chapters of Ephesians speak on how the Church's foundation is built on the apostles and prophets, with Jesus Christ as the chief cornerstone. Some interpret this as a reference to the Old Testament prophets, which is certainly valid. But talk of this foundation is followed in Ephesians 4:11 with a description and purpose of the fivefold ministry given by Christ to His Church: apostles, prophets, evangelists, pastors, and teachers. The next two verses read that the fivefold ministry gifts will remain until the Church is brought into full unity, maturity, and intimacy. The fact that the Church has yet to reach this point means that all God's prophetic giftings are still valid.

What is it like to be a forerunner? At times, you will feel like a person born ahead of his time. You will feel as though you are carrying and incubating that which is beforehand. This can create a certain amount of tension, which is why it is so important to avoid the pitfalls of pride, alienation, isolation, and rejection. You have received a message ahead of time. Why? So you can help prepare a people, respond in prayer, and aid in ushering in whatever God wants to do in that time and place.

Another function of revelatory graces is to help prepare the Church to be both the Bride of Christ and the army of God— it's to make ready a people prepared for the Lord. The Bride of Christ must be fully clothed in her wedding garments and fully equipped with her weapons, such as the Word of God. Where Ephesians 6:17 talks about taking up the sword of the Spirit, which is the Word of God, the Greek word for "word" is *rhema*, which refers to God's spoken word. The Lord wants to release His revelatory graces, so that they become a sword in the Spirit to cut off the enemy.

Prophetic ministry helps activate individual Christians into their own ministries and functions. The prophetic anointing releases the creative ability to impart, birth, and activate specific ministries into individuals. It is used to stir up giftings and ignite faith, hope, and love; it's like spiritual jumper cables that transfer a power surge of God's presence from one person to the next and charges them up with spiritual courage to accomplish the task.

What is the purpose of revelatory graces? They help us follow Christ Jesus and become more like Him. Revelation 19:10b says, "For the testimony of Jesus is the spirit of prophecy." Jesus is the express image of the Father. Everything about Jesus is a testimony of the Father's true nature and will. Our prophetic ministry today should be a testimony of the "Good News" of Jesus in word, attitude, and deed. As our knowledge of Jesus increases through the prophetic message, then grace and peace will be multiplied in our daily lives. Let's thank the Lord together!

15

⁓

The Revelation of the New Anointing

YE SHALL know the truth, and the truth shall make you free (John 8:32). One of the greatest truths that God has ever revealed to me—for fighting and for winning every time, in the great spiritual warfare in which we are engaged—is the revelation of the New Anointing. This revelation not only has revolutionized my life and ministry, but it has done so to the lives and ministries of countless ministers and Christian leaders around the world with whom I have shared this teaching.

I have testimony after testimony on file of people (literally thousands) who have learned these truths and have applied them in their own lives to witness the most amazing answers to prayers that they have ever known. Using these truths, they have prayed in the Spirit to grasp victories that have eluded them for years.

Romans 8:26 Likewise the Spirit also helpeth our infirmities: for we know not what we should pray for as we ought: but the Spirit itself maketh intercession for us with groanings which cannot be uttered.

I have experienced that. I found, instead of dealing with the things on the surface, I was dealing with the root cause in the spirit world.

The anguish I would go through in prayer in order to win victories in America was indescribable. I would travail intensely in prayer because I knew I was combating special demonic forces. I was coming to grips with the supernatural powers of the archenemy, Satan. I knew that these powers had to be defeated in prayer before I ever left the prayer room.

As I travailed and prevailed in prayer in that hotel room, God spoke to my heart in a very unusual way. He said to me, *"Son, you must realize that in the United States of America, in North America, you are not dealing just with ideologies. You are not just dealing with rebellious youth who are disenchanted with the hypocrisy of their parents. You are not just dealing with kids who are trying to tear down the establishment. You are not just dealing with the drug culture or the gay movement. If you will go deep to the root of the problem, you will find that you are in a spiritual battle."*

He revealed to my heart that there were tremendous spirit forces working in North America to tear down the very structure of our society. I believe with all my heart that the devil has assigned special spirits to the task of destroying North America. God showed me explicitly that the key used for such victories on the foreign field, the spiritual binding and defeating of satanic power in the arena of prayer, was the key for victories in North America, just as it had been in the other countries of the world. The warfare was the same.

On the other side is the great news that we know how to deal victoriously with Satan and we are going to do it. The Bible, God's voice to us, is our real training manual. We can rely upon the Word of God and the Spirit of God to defeat Satan every time, not only in our own lives, but in the lives of our loved ones.

No war is pleasant. No warfare is pretty, spiritual warfare less so than all others. We must stop playing patty-cake with the devil. "Pretty" prayers will never do the job. We must see past our "civilization," our "education," and our "sophistication." We must see the terrors of this warfare and realize what it is we need to combat it. We must learn to press our way through in the Spirit, to the very stronghold of Satan and tear from his grasp the victories of which he has robbed us all these years. We not only must learn it, we must do it!

We must press the battle until every skirmish is over, every victory is ours, until we are more than conquerors in every situation as God has promised we will be: *"In all these things we are more than conquerors through him that loved us"* (Romans 8:37)

We can do it. We will do it as we understand the battle plan and as we move out into the arena of conflict under God's provision and leadership. We must do it, for if something doesn't happen, and soon, the world is on a collision course of spiritual annihilation.

The time has come for God to give you a New Anointing.

16

⚛

The Secret of Spiritual Strength

You know sometimes God has secrets that are not really a secret. They are secrets because most people are not seeking the face of God. At this point, I know that you have a deep desire to be freed from every one of your fears. But by now you are also aware that if you are ever going to gain victory over fear, there's going to be a fight! Spiritual battles take energy—energy which you don't think you have right now.

I'm now going to show you the reason why you have not been able to press through to victory in your battles against fear. It is because it takes spiritual energy to stand and fight. Spiritual battles cannot be fought in natural strength. Inside, your spiritual well has run dry. Therefore, you've fallen into the habit of retreating or compromising in defeat.

This is what is called a defensive position in warfare. A defensive position doesn't take any energy at all; an offensive position does. You have been too bound by fear to get in touch with God's power within you and fight offensively.

So how do you tap into His abundant energy? There is only one secret to real spiritual strength.

In the Bible, God promises us that,

Romans 8:31, 32 What shall we then say to these things? If God *be* for us, who *can be* against us? He that spared not his own Son, but delivered him up for us all, how shall he not with him also freely give us all things?

Notice that in the first half of His instructions, God establishes a prerequisite for freedom. That prerequisite is, "if you abide in My Word." In other words, if you do your part by living in total obedience to His Word, then you shall know the truth, and within the truth itself is all the strength and power you need to be fully free.

So the first question I want to ask you is: "Are you abiding daily in His Word?" Next, let me ask you: "If it is the truth itself which makes us free, what is the truth?"

Somebody said to me, "The truth is the Word of God."

That is correct, but the Word of God is more than just a written Book. The Word is also the living Word—who is Jesus Christ Himself! *"In the beginning was the Word, and the Word was with God, and the Word was God"* (John 1:1).

The Living Word, Jesus, is Himself the living Truth. He said, *"I am the way, the truth, and the life..."* (John 14:6). Therefore, it is the combination of your knowledge of the written Word, combined with your knowledge of the living Word and the living Truth (Jesus Christ) dwelling within you, which is the Source of all spiritual strength!

For years, many of you have been faithfully building a good spiritual foundation through your knowledge of the written Word. You know all about God's plan of salvation, His Great Commission, the keys of binding and loosing, the "Four Spiritual Laws," and everything else.

But those of you who have been paralyzed by fear have not built an equally firm foundation of personal knowledge and the personal experience of Him living within you. Your relationship with Him has been weak; therefore, your spiritual strength has also been weak. Because you have not been in touch daily with the experience of Christ within you, you have not been free.

You may know a lot about Him through His written Word, but if you don't know Him personally, your spiritual "house" will eventually crumble. He Himself warns, *"...without me ye can do nothing"* (John 15:5). The Pharisees of Jesus' day had to face this same issue when Jesus told them:

John 5:39, 40 Search the scriptures; for in them ye think ye have eternal life: and they are they which testify of me. And ye will not come to me, that ye might have life.

Freedom from fear takes spiritual strength, the kind of strength that can only be drawn from getting in touch with Christ in you, your hope of glory! (See Colossians 1:27.) In the most famous chapter on spiritual warfare ever written, the apostle Paul says:

Ephesians 6:10 Finally, my brethren, be strong in the Lord, and in the power of his might.

Remember that five of the ten ladies in Matthew 25 did not have the spiritual strength to make it to the wedding feast. Their lamps had run dry. Why? Until they actually stood face to face with the Lord, they had assumed they were in good shape. Instead, they were cast out. Why didn't they have the strength to make it in the end?

The Lord gave them the answer. He said, *"...I know you not"* (Matthew 25:12). Obviously, they knew His written Word, and they had gone out to meet Him. *But they had not spent their lives getting to know Him.* The most precious talent He gives us is our *time,* and they had not invested it wisely!

I beg you to be aware that it is only through a powerful, personal union with Him that you will ever come to know the true Source of spiritual strength. He is about to give you a breakthrough into the true knowledge of Him, which is the basis of that union. It is a union of strength. It is the union of His love.

Several years ago, God revealed to me that all truth is parallel. By this, I mean that man lives in two worlds—the natural realm and the spiritual realm. Nothing happens in one world that doesn't have a parallel effect in the other. In our natural world we are seeing astounding things take place daily. Breakthroughs in science and technology that were considered science fiction only 50 years ago are now becoming commonplace.

What is a breakthrough? A breakthrough is a sudden burst of advanced knowledge. It is that sudden burst of revelation where, with a surge of insight, you suddenly look up and say, "I've got it!"

But if all truth is parallel, and these things are happening in the natural world, what is going on in the spiritual world and in the lives of born-again Christians? I'll tell you. Right now, God is pouring out His Spirit in a new work of grace and total restoration, deep in your inner self. He is taking you into a new spiritual dimension of revelation.

The revelation of His Son in you! Remember that our definition of revelation has been "the drawing away of the veil of darkness." Until now you have been in darkness concerning His life, His love, and His power within you. God is about to give you a breakthrough into the true knowledge of Him dwelling in your heart.

Believe me, revelation is power! You will learn to both recognize and break through to His Presence within you. Empowered by His love, you will rise up in a new spirit of victory that will cause all fear to flee.

Let me explain. Throughout the Bible, God has always had two ways of doing things. The first way has been to work from outside His people, bestowing His blessings upon them—in other words, to do things for them. The second way has been to work in and through them from the inside out.

As an illustration, look at His plan of salvation. Salvation itself is a two-fold process. First is the work of salvation which Christ accomplished for us through His life, death, and resurrection. Second is the work that God wants to do within us through His Holy Spirit, empowering us from the inside out. The first part of salvation is the outward work of God, done for us. The second is His inward work, done within us.

For too long, people in the Church have been stuck in a rut, empty of inner power, because they have been focusing all of their attention on what they wanted God to do *for* them and ignoring the powerful work that He longs to do *in* them. Thousands of people have come crying to the altar: "Oh, God, I can't get deliverance. Give me the victory over fear."

But God is telling them, "I put My Son, Jesus, inside you." "...*Greater is he that is in you, than he that is in the world*" (1 John 4:4). Stand up on your feet. Call on God. Fix your faith on Him. Let go of those fears, and let Him rise up against them. Let Him expel them from the inside out. When you do, you will never be the same.

For years I've been saying that it's time for the Church to move beyond the point of blessing (what God wants to do for you) into the realm of power (what He wants to do within you). This is what I've been talking about. Right now, God wants you to have a breakthrough whereby you stop viewing His grace as simply an outward blessing or favor and come into the experience of it as the power of Christ within you, the only power that can overcome all fear. If you have any doubts about God's grace as an actual power or spiritual force within you, listen to what our Lord told the apostle Paul about the famous thorn in his life. Three times Paul had asked the Lord to remove it (to do all the work for him from the outside). But the Lord told him, *"...My grace is sufficient for thee: for my strength is made perfect in weakness..."* (2 Corinthians 12:9).

Believe me, the Lord was not referring to His grace as some type of passive blessing. He was referring to it as a formidable inward force. It is His assistance within us which, when exercised by Paul, would strengthen him until the apostle—in union with the Lord— could overcome any foe!

This is the very force that God Himself is placing within you now to give you all of the breakthrough power you need to completely defeat fear.

Romans 6:14 For sin shall not have dominion over you: for ye are not under the law, but under grace.

With God's new work of revelation and His new outpouring of grace in your heart, you will now have all of the assistance you need in your inner man to be dead to all fears and alive only to Christ. You will begin to discover for yourself, *"nevertheless I live; yet not I, but Christ liveth in me"* (Galatians 2:20). His astounding love for you will soon begin to break through all of the walls you have built out of fear. It will soon penetrate and rule all of your thoughts.

This is what it means to be renewed in the spirit of your mind (see Ephesians 4:23). All spirits of fear and darkness will be cast out, and the Spirit of God will be in, ruling all you do.

You ask, "When will all of this start taking place in my life?" It will start the moment you agree to stand on your feet and begin saying no to the spirit of fear! That is why this is an important growth period for you. It is a time when you will finally begin to:

Isaiah 35:3 Strengthen ye the weak hands, and confirm the feeble knees.

Hebrews 12:12, 13 Wherefore lift up the hands which hang down, and the feeble knees; And make straight paths for your feet, lest that which is lame be turned out of the way; but let it rather be healed.

This is also a time when our Lord is asking us to, "...*be on the watch to look [after one another], to see that no one falls back from and fails to secure God's grace...*" (Hebrews 12:15 AMP). Beloved, once you have begun to stand up and lay hold of God's grace within you, there is one more aspect of your personal relationship with Him that you must understand if you are to maintain total victory over fear.

17

~

Time to Tune In

Have you ever heard a news cast say stay tuned? This is because something special is coming. We "tune" some-thing "to bring into harmony; to adjust for precise functioning; to make more precise, intense, or effective." I don't know about you, but something inside me wants to be in harmony with the Creator of the universe! I want Him to adjust me however He needs to, so that I will function with precision, intensity, and effectiveness!

We all need to "tune in," but most of us treat it as a one-time necessity. The fact is that our spirits need to be constantly fine-tuned to the heart of God. Who would drive a car month after month and year after year without ever giving it a tune-up? What orchestra would tune its instruments at the beginning of the year and then perform every concert based on that one tuning? It's the same with us in the Spirit. If we don't tune in regularly, we will drift off the station, just like an old radio playing static.

Have you ever felt as if God has changed His "channel" on you? Being human and creatures of habit, we get used to always hearing God in the same way. We act as though He is not allowed to change His methods—it's as if we are in charge! Once we realize that our "receiving set" isn't working anymore, we point our finger at God: "I'm just not hearing God like I used to. I don't understand what He's doing. I just don't understand what He's saying anymore. I'm not hearing Him."

Sometimes, I think that God shakes His head at our inflexibility and says, "Okay, I'm going to stretch you a little bit. It's time to change the channel. I know you hear Me very well in the clean atmosphere of a worship service. Let Me switch My stream to another channel that requires an inquiring heart boosted with tenacity in the middle of a cluttered day. Let's see if you can make that adjustment." This process of "tuning in" and focusing on the Lord, regardless of circumstance, is vital to our growth in Christ.

The Bible says the natural man does not receive the things of the Spirit of God. we can turn that dial all the way to the left then go slowly over every station...but as long as we are on, we are not going to receive His message because the natural man is receiving. The key is to be spiritually discerning—to open our spirit man to direct revelation from God.

But there is another side to this "tuning" process. High-fidelity radio and precision radar systems lock in on desired frequencies and also tune out extraneous noise or "ground clutter."

In the same way, we need to develop our ability to tune in God's voice at all times but also be able to tune out distractions that block His still, small voice. This "fine-tuning" process isn't a rapid one, but it builds the character and heart of God into our lives. We need to learn how to "tune out" all voices of criticism, doubt, unbelief, negativity, and gossip that bombard us every day!

One of the most vital ingredients in relationships with our mechanic, pastor, or personal physician is honesty. After all, none of those people can help us if they don't have honest facts about our condition. An honest evaluation is the first step to any "tune-up." God will examine us to see what work needs to be done, so we don't need to worry that He will be shocked by any of our revelations. He won't stomp off if we tell Him that we're upset, disappointed, burned out, or even angry. He already knows about all of that—it won't surprise Him one bit. He's just waiting for us to tell Him.

Now, I'm not talking about having a "gripe session," although I do confess to having had a few of those with Him. God patiently listens until we run out of steam! Then He releases a trickle of His anointing oil to bring healing and grace into our heart. That's when we respond, "God, I am angry, and I don't want to be this way. Will You help me?" God wants us to be honest, so that He can clean out our spiritual "pipeline." Sometimes, we get so busy that we don't know how much junk is clogging up our lifeline to the Father. Don't be afraid to be honest with the Lord. Open up to Him completely.

When you get frustrated, take time to ask yourself, "Okay, what is good? What has Father God done for me?" This may be difficult at first because we all tend to get very self-absorbed during these "down times." Don't give in to that temptation. Make the decision to turn away from ungodliness, and openly make confessions to God. This releases God's power in your heart to clean you out and also helps you step from a limited place of frustration into His spacious place of grace and loving acceptance. Honesty frees you to become Heaven- and eternity-minded. I love what Hebrews says,

Hebrews 12:1-4 Wherefore seeing we also are compassed about with so great a cloud of witnesses, let us lay aside every weight, and the sin which doth so easily beset *us,* and let us run with patience the race that is set before us, Looking unto Jesus the author and finisher of *our* faith; who for the joy that was set before him endured the cross, despising the shame, and is set down at the right hand of the throne of God. For consider him that endured such contradiction of sinners against himself, lest ye be wearied and faint in your minds. Ye have not yet resisted unto blood, striving against sin.

When God revealed this Scripture passage, I became totally disarmed. He was saying, "Don't grow weary; don't faint; be strong." We can be encouraged from understanding what Jesus bore in His earthly life. Become strengthened by meditating on everything that Jesus did for us.

In a world full of obstacles, controversy, and occasional sorrows, we sometimes reach a point when our efforts to tune in to God just aren't enough. After suffering a major blow, we sometimes feel "knocked out of adjustment" and in need of heavy-duty maintenance. The Holy Spirit wants to have free reign in us. We may believe ourselves to be on the cutting edge of faith, but if we continue yielding to the Spirit of God, our future adventures in Him will be overwhelming. Where we are today will seem infantile compared to the days to come. If we allow God to tune us up, and learn to tune in to His tender whisper and tune out distractions, then we will truly discover life in an atmosphere of radical faith.

God wants to bring new definitions to what we have yet to even contemplate. Today, you and I may believe, "Well, my engine feels like it's running pretty good." But we don't know everything that lies ahead a few miles down the road, or fully know what race God has assigned us to. We might come to a sharp, snake turn or need new brake pads to keep from losing control on a mountain road or to avoid a collision. We all need a few tune-ups from time to time—not just for today, but for tomorrow as well.

In all situations, we should tune in to that one great song of the universe: Jesus Christ. He is the sound of the universe, the Word who was in the beginning with God and who was God (see John 1:1). Every aspect of Paul's admonition in Philippians 4:8 (KJV) focuses on the pride and joy of the Father: "Whatsoever things are true, whatsoever things are honest, whatsoever things are just, whatsoever things are pure, whatsoever things are lovely, whatsoever things are of good report, if there be any virtue, and if there be any praise, think on these things." Can you think of anyone more lovely, more pure, or more honest than Jesus Himself? Who is more virtuous or praiseworthy than Jesus? Who has been more faithful than He, or more gracious, or more forgiving?

Years ago, the Lord set me on a path of instruction and began teaching me how to train my thoughts. Along the way, He led me to the parable of the sower of the seed in chapter 8 of the Gospel of Luke. As I read the first verse, which says, "The sower went out to sow his seed..." (Luke 8:5), I felt as if I was reading the passage for the very first time. The Lord is sowing His seed—the Word of God—in us, even as we read these words:

Luke 8:5-8 A sower went out to sow his seed: and as he sowed, some fell by the way side; and it was trodden down, and the fowls of the air devoured it. And some fell upon a rock; and as soon as it was sprung up, it withered away, because it lacked moisture. And some fell among thorns; and the thorns sprang up with it, and choked it. And other fell on good ground, and sprang up, and bare fruit an hundredfold. And when he had said these things, he cried, He that hath ears to hear, let him hear.

In Luke 8:11, Jesus explains to His disciples that the Word of God is "the seed" in this parable. When I read that Scripture, I realized that I always considered this verse to be a "salvation" passage—one that referred to lost people hearing the gospel. The Lord refocused my understanding to see that He is continually sowing His Word in us as He plants direction, deliverance, and guidance in our lives. Consider the Lord's own interpretation of His parable,

Luke 8:12-18 Those by the way side are they that hear; then cometh the devil, and taketh away the word out of their hearts, lest they should believe and be saved. They on the rock *are they,* which, when they hear, receive the word with joy; and these have no root, which for a while believe, and in time of temptation fall away. And that which fell among thorns are they, which, when they have heard, go forth, and are choked with cares and riches and pleasures of *this* life, and bring no fruit to perfection. But that on the good ground are they, which in an honest and good heart, having heard the word, keep *it,* and bring forth fruit with patience. No man, when he hath lighted a candle, covereth it with a vessel, or putteth *it* under a bed; but setteth *it* on a candlestick, that they which enter in may see the light. For nothing is secret, that shall not be made manifest; neither *any thing* hid, that shall not be known and come abroad. Take heed therefore how ye hear: for whosoever hath, to him shall be given; and whosoever hath not, from him shall be taken even that which he seemeth to have.

There is a difference between hearing and listening. Hearing merely requires the physical ability to detect sound; but listening involves the mind in the natural realm and the heart in the spiritual realm. I believe that is why Jesus said over and over again, "He who has ears to hear, let him hear." Virtually every-one around Him had the physical ability to hear, but only a few "had ears to hear," which meant they had the desire to listen and receive what He said. Now is the time for the Church to be "all ears"! Begin to listen from the heart.

You can *hear* and still ignore. *Listening* to the Holy Spirit's voice is an attitude and action of the heart. You poise your heart in such a way that you are *always* trying to hear God. You wait in a positive, eager posture. You have a certain confidence that God is going to speak, and you tune your ear to hear His slightest whisper. God's voice can come suddenly at times, but if you "have ears to hear," then His voice will hit your ear with such power that it "takes your breath away" and jars you out of automatic mode.

At other times, you will barely hear a gentle whisper in the wind. Yet, this still, small voice will bypass your ears and sink deep into your spirit. In the words of Eliphaz the Temanite, "Now a word was brought to me stealthily, and my ear received a whisper of it" (Job 4:12). Very often, the Holy Spirit speaks so softly that He gives you just enough to prompt the question, "What was that? Was that You, Lord?"

God is teaching us how to posture ourselves for a lifestyle of listening. We don't want to miss a single whisper from His beloved lips! So be careful how you listen, for it can make all the difference in your life in Christ. Listen to the good and ignore the bad. As David wrote in the Psalms, as he spoke prophetically of Jesus Christ: "Thou hast loved righteousness, and hated wickedness; therefore God, Thy God, has anointed Thee with the oil of joy above Thy fellows" (Ps. 45:7). Be careful how you listen.

We all have times when we don't seem to hear from God. These dry times may come because of doubt and disbelief or because we haven't made a strong commitment to Jesus Christ as Lord. Some of us go through dry times because we are hiding unconfessed sin or living a "double standard" life. The solution in these cases should be obvious: Oh, call on the blood of Jesus! At other times, some are unaware of scriptural evidence proving our right and privilege to hear from God personally. A lack of teaching on how to pursue such a listening prayer experience can also be a hindrance. Others are simply afraid of being led astray by the enemy. I have good news, there is a better way.

If you can say "Yes!" to these statements, then rest assured that God is speaking to you!

1. What I heard helps me to respect the Lord with a godly fear, and to depart from evil (see Job 28:28).
2. The message I received from God increases my faith in His Word, as well as my knowledge and understanding of it (see Proverbs 4:7).

1. When I obey what God told me to do, the results produce one or more of the spiritual fruits of purity, peace, gentleness, mercy, courtesy, good deeds, and sincerity without hypocrisy (see James 3:17).
2. What I heard strengthens me "with all power" so that I can keep going no matter what happens (see Colossians 1:11).
3. These words cause me to experience joyfulness and thanksgiving to the Father (see Col. 1:12).

1. Don't make it complicated. It's hard not to hear God if you really want to please and obey Him! Follow three simple steps that will help you hear His voice:
    1. Submit to His Lordship. Ask Him to help you silence your own thoughts and desires, and the opinions of others. You only want to hear the thoughts of the Lord (see Proverbs 3:5-6).
    2. Resist the enemy. Use the authority given to you by Jesus Christ to silence the enemy's voice (see James 4:7; Ephesians 6:10-20).
    3. Ask whatever question is on your mind and wait for Him to answer. If you expect your loving, heavenly Fa-

ther to speak to you, He will (see John 10:27; Psalms 69:13; Exodus 33:11).

1. Allow God to speak however He chooses. Don't tell Him how to guide you. If you listen with a yielded heart, then you will hear Him. He may choose to speak to you through:
    1. His Word.
    2. An audible voice.
    3. Dreams and visions.
    4. The quiet inner voice, which is probably the most common of all His methods (see Isaiah 30:21).
2. Confess any known sins; a clean heart is a prerequisite to hearing God (see Psalms 66:18).
3. Always obey the last command God gave. Ask yourself, "Have I obeyed the last word God told me to do?"
4. Get your own leading. God will use others to confirm your guidance, but you should also hear from Him directly (see 1 Kings 13).
5. Don't talk about your word too soon. Refrain from sharing your guidance until God gives you permission to do so. The main purpose of waiting is to help you avoid four pitfalls: pride; presumption; missing God's timing and method; and bringing confusion to others.
6. Know that God will confirm what He's telling you. Expect confirmation. God will often use two or more spiritually sensitive people to confirm the message He has given to you (see 2 Corinthians 13:1).
7. Beware of counterfeits. Satan has a counterfeit for everything of God that it is possible for him to copy (see Acts 8:9-11).

1. Practice hearing God's voice. The more you practice doing so, the easier the process becomes. It's similar to picking up the tele-

phone and recognizing a friend's voice—you know his or her voice because you've heard it so much.

10. Cultivate an intimate relationship with the Lord. Relationship is the most important reason for hearing the voice of God. If you don't communicate with Him, then you don't have a personal relationship. True guidance comes from getting closer to the Guide. We grow to know the Lord better as He speaks to us. As we listen to Him and obey, we make His heart glad (see Exodus 33:11; Matthews 7:24-27).

One way God speaks to us is through dream encounters. There will be seasons when God speaks to you on certain subjects through dreams. By recording your dreams, you can review them; as you progress in your walk with Christ, you will gain greater understanding into their meaning.

One of the most important keys in hearing God's voice is to learn the value of silence. We've all heard the old saying, "Silence is golden," and it is so true. Quieting our soul before the Lord tunes us in to His golden Presence. The practice of being quiet in God's presence is an art that is all but lost in our fast-paced, modern society. We must take time to relearn this ancient, almost forgotten spiritual discipline.

How are you when it comes to silence? Do you find being on your own quite natural and enjoyable? Or are you uncomfortable being quiet? If you struggle with being alone, don't give up; you are not a failure. Before you try spending time alone and in silence for the first time, understand something: If you have been running from inner fears and insecurities and then try to sit in silence, you are going to continue running for a while. Your soul will need time to slow down and become quiet. Give yourself whatever time you need. Many people use activity and busyness to avoid facing the deeper questions of life. Some of us are cluttered inside with years of accumulated hopes and fears, plans and ideas, and a mixture of light and darkness. The Holy Spirit often has to clear space before He can accomplish His wonderful work of healing and restoration.

Perhaps a healing encounter awaits you? Multitudes of people have experienced crippling hurts and wounds. I don't care how old you are or what has happened in your life; the Lord wants to heal every hurt and wound within your heart and mind. Your Father wants to put His healing ointment on your heart. Whether you've been on the receiving or giving end of hurt, God's love is available. Perhaps you feel as if you have missed an opportunity with your kids by being too harsh or insensitive toward them. The point is simply this: Grace, love, and forgiveness is waiting for you in God's hand.

You may not realize it now, but when the Father sweeps His love over you, He often uncovers lots of hidden wounds that have left you imprisoned. After the Spirit has brought such a release, the enemy often raises questions to bring turmoil and conflict. The cure is simple and effective: "Whatsoever things are true, and honest, and of a good report, if there be any virtue, or any praise, think on these things." We must graft the good Word of God into our soul to cleanse, heal, restore, and save us. This procedure is necessary to tune our hearts to hear His voice. These simple points of listening—slowing down, quieting our soul, and grafting in the Word of God—are essential if we are to cooperate with the process of healing hurts that hinder hearing God's voice.

Do you feel like an unlikely candidate to receive personal revelation from God? I've got news for you: God *wants* us to be a people of revelation! We don't have to beg Him because He wants to give it more than we want to receive. He passionately wants to light the "lamp of revelation" in our hearts (see 1 Samual 3:1-3; 2 Kings 6:17; Daniel 12:3; John 16:13-15). The first step for us is to simply ask!

We need to believe that Peter was talking about us when he stood up in Jerusalem on the Day of Pentecost and quoted the prophecy of Joel. He meant you and me when he said "sons and daughters" would prophesy, and young men would see visions, old men would dream dreams, and men and women would prophesy (see Acts 2:17-18).

According to Peter, dreams, visions, and revelation are all scriptural; they are for us—all of us—and are for today. Our job is to ask and receive according to James 4:2 and John 16:24. Do you want the spirit of wisdom and revelation? Then ask!

How does revelation come? It comes in answer to prayer (see 1 Kings 3:3-5; Daniel 2:17-19), in special situations (see Genesis 28:10-12; Matthew 2:19), and in response to fasting (see Daniel 9–10). God has commanded each of us to "set our minds and affections on things above," or on the things of Heaven and of our Father (see Romans 8:5-9; 12:1-2; Colossians 3:1-2). Once again, I must emphasize that quietness is the "incubation cradle" for revelation. God is quite clear that quietness is one of the necessities of receiving revelation from Him. He will not compete for our attention, but He does demand it as a condition for hearing His voice (see Psalms 46:10; 131:1-3; Isaiah 30:15). We must be cradled in His love, which casts out fear, and lean our head on His heart. Quietness is a great key to unlocking the spirit of revelation in our life.

We can learn from the wisdom of those who have success-fully and consistently heard from God in their own lives. These people stand out from the crowd because their lives bear the fruit of God's presence and anointing. Here are excerpts from the writings and journals of some of these people:

If these men and women could cultivate an intimate lifestyle of continuous communion with God, then so can you. God is not a "respecter" of persons; He loves and responds to each one of us the same way—with great joy and delight. On our part, we need to take some very practical steps to make sure we don't hinder the flow of pure revelation from God's heart into our own.

We need to walk in the Spirit of God and live in a godly fashion. The Bible compares the lives of those who don't follow God to the waters of a troubled sea always kicking up dirt and debris (see Isaiah 57:20-21). We need to guard our hearts and make sure that worries do not dominate our thinking and our actions. The solution is to cast all our cares upon Jesus because He cares for us (see Psalms 37:8; 1 Peter 5:7). The same is true of anger, lust, bitterness from unforgiveness, and addictions of any kind (see Ephesians 4:26; Romans 13:10-14; Hebrews 12:15; Ephesians 5:18, respectively). This special attention to our lifestyle even extends to our choices for entertainment and how much leisure we seek (see Mark 4:24). Maintaining a consistent schedule of prayer, meditation, work, and play in our lives also helps. But the most important and effective change we can make to hear God's voice is to ask Him to speak!

If asking God to speak seems intimidating, have no fear! He wants us to ask! God wants to speak to us! That's the way we build a relationship with our heavenly Father. God wants us to hear His voice even more than we want to hear it. And the way we hear Him is through a relationship.... *We must cultivate a love relationship with the Father God.* We hear Him when we pray. We hear Him by reading His written Word. We hear Him because we are sons and daughters in relationship with our awesome Father. No gifting can ever take the place of a relationship. A love relationship with our Father God through Jesus Christ is the foundation of all true communion.

We must each realize a very elementary yet important aspect: God likes to speak to His kids! How do we hear? We hear because of His great grace set toward us. We hear because He speaks loudly enough and well enough for us to catch it. We hear because He pursues us. He wants us to hear His voice more than we want to hear it!

Isaiah 50:4, 5 The Lord GOD hath given me the tongue of the learned, that I should know how to speak a word in season to *him that is* weary: he wakeneth morning by morning, he wakeneth mine ear to hear as the learned. The Lord GOD hath opened mine ear, and I was not rebellious, neither turned away back.

The Lord will open your ear. He will awaken the interest of your heart to enable you to listen. He will come morning after morning and night after night to pursue you with His great love. How do you hear God's voice? He helps you! How will you encounter His beckoning call? By grace! Do you want to have a "listening encounter" with God?

18

~

VISION AND VALUES

Luke 12:24 Consider the ravens: for they neither sow nor reap; which neither have storehouse nor barn; and God feedeth them: how much more are ye better than the fowls?

Jesus called His disciples to enter into service in the Kingdom. They each made a profound faith connection with His simple words, "*come follow me*". The disciples believed Jesus was calling them into a ministry of faith; all ministry must be faith orientated or it is only works. Ministry and ministerial partnership must be Christ-centred and inspired by the Holy Spirit.

The Kingdom of God is built on values, which are the foundation for Kingdom vision. It is important that partnership echoes this sentiment. In order for people to "buy in" to vision it must be clearly communicated in order to be understood and agreed upon. Effective communication built on shared faith in Christ and His Kingdom is a powerful tool in partnership allowing potential partners to 'buy in' to the specifics of the ministry vision. The phrase 'buy in' in no way implies a financial exchange but rather expresses active involvement and agreement between the concerned parties.

The Kingdom of God is pro-citizenship! Jesus said, "Blessed are the poor in spirit, for theirs is the kingdom of heaven." Matthew 5:3 The

Apostle Paul echoed Christ's sentiments in his words to the church at Philippi, *"But our citizenship is in heaven."* Philippians 3:20

• Belonging is at the core of our faith and is an important aspect of partnering with a ministry vision.

• Identification of values and commonality of faith in Jesus Christ births a unique sense of belonging in the hearts of individuals and groups of people.

• People develop a sense of ownership when they feel as though they belong.

• Ownership births commitment to Godly stewardship

• Godly stewardship develops our characters and tests/trains our talents – burden bearing teaches us about responsibility, sharing, caring, etc.

• Relationship is everything - works and witness flow from walking with the Lord

God loves us too much to allow us to remain in the same condition as when we first met Him. In other words, the Kingdom is about Godly change in our lives that leads to transformation. Discipleship is a process; a journey we take with Jesus and each other. Belief, buy in and belonging in the importance of Kingdom values will manifest in the production, consolidation, implementation and completion of strategic Kingdom vision both on an individual and corporate basis. Apostle Paul wrote to the Ephesians that leaders are to equip the saints for the work of the ministry (Ephesians 4:12). When people partner with us in Godly vision we must place a high value on them not only as partners from whom we may receive but also as individuals whose leadership potential we are privileged to invest in and develop.

Charles H. Spurgeon wrote, "To do the Lord's work must be as necessary as food to us. His Father's work is that in which we also are engaged, and we cannot do better than imitate our Lord. Tell me, then, how Jesus set about it. Did He set about it by arranging to build a huge Tabernacle, or by organizing a monster conference, or by publishing a great book, or by sounding a trumpet before Him in any other form? Did He aim at something great, and altogether out of the common line of service? Did

He bid high for popularity, and wear Himself out by an exhausting exaggeration. No; He called disciples to Him one by one, and instructed each one with patient care."

Matthew 5:1, 2 And seeing the multitudes, he went up into a mountain: and when he was set, his disciples came unto him: And he opened his mouth, and taught them, saying, When Jesus went up on to the mountain He provided us with a blueprint for establishing Godly partnership. Partnership is revealed at various levels as we study the Lord's interaction with the three, the twelve, the seventy two and the multitudes. In this instance Jesus reveals partnership to us both on micro and macro level:

• Jesus was sharing His Kingdom vision and values and teaching His inner circle of disciples, i.e. team (who were partners with Him in the Kingdom)

• At the same time as training His team, Jesus was also influencing a whole new group of potential Kingdom associates on the mount!

The Lord demonstrates how it is possible to have an inner core partnership team in training at the same time as reaching the multitudes of unsaved potential people partners around us. Jesus modeled and taught perfect leadership. When Jesus was on the mountain: *"He saw"*

Jesus saw the crowds and because His heart was attuned to His Father's He saw with His Father's perspective and responded as an obedient Son. Jesus saw the Kingdom potential in each one of the people before Him, most especially those whom He was training in His inner circle. I believe that every person has some leadership capability within them and that leadership can be "caught" as well as being taught. Jesus saw this promise in His twelve and many others too. As you outwork vision you will discover potential in everyone with whom you partner. Be willing to love your team with God's unconditional love. Love with expectancy but without condition. Our attitude to the multitudes must be the same as Christ Jesus, who loves us one heart at a time with dignity, equality and respect. As leaders of churches and ministries, we are entrusted with the role of pressing in to the Father for divine direction. Our relationship with our Heavenly Father is pivotal to our response to His people. Jesus spent time alone with His Father; He also studied the Scriptures and took responsibility for His own leadership development and so must we.

Before we can bring vision down from the heavenly realms to the earth, we must first ascend into the Father's presence.

• We must birth plans from a heavenly perspective and not an earthly viewpoint

• We should flow in the Spirit of wisdom and revelation;

• A good leader must be committed to personal development, education and training. Ministry is a posture in son ship, not a 'position'.

A 'position mentality' will have us hanging to the coat tails of men, whilst a 'posture mentality' will have us touching the hem of the garment of Christ. Posture is about relational reality with Father, Son and Holy Spirit.

Posture n. 1. A particular position of the body; the way in which a person holds their body;

2. An approach or attitude towards something When we are postured as sons, the only Person we will promote is the Father, His love and His work.

Position –a place where someone or something is located or has been put. When we are more concerned about position than son ship, it promotes a hierarchical mind-set in which a person is more focused on who they are than who God is!

When this occurs there is a danger of self-glorification rather than living to glorify God, which can lead to striving, manipulations and control. Ministry is a privilege we are entrusted with by God's grace. Every person is a partner with heaven because of their relationship with Christ. Every partner has something valuable in God to contribute to Kingdom ministry.

Intimacy with the Lord is the key to harvest and when we come from His presence we have fresh manna to share with those whom we encounter. Sitting down with God involves quiet time, worship, prayer and study of the Scriptures. It includes waiting with Jesus and learning to "be" rather than always be involved in the activity of "doing". Stillness before God precedes strategy and intimacy with Him will produce a harvest of fruitfulness; we will reproduce who and what we are – either fullness in Christ or the emptiness of flesh and self. Leaders are busy people and it is essential that we make time to be with the Lord so that we do not end up running on empty. Jesus did not keep the intimacy He enjoyed with His Father to Himself. He lived to give and so must we. The Lord was willing to sit down with both His disciples and also the multitudes. A fruit of being in God's presence is that we are able to overflow with His love to others. Jesus brought people together into Kingdom connectedness because of His presence. He birthed Kingdom vision through His lifestyle and His words. He lived as a son serving His Father and so must we.

Jesus mentored His inner circle, training them and raising them up as a loving father would raise his own sons. To train someone is to teach them a task, which is a necessary part of accomplishing duties. To raise someone as a son (or daughter) is to be willing to weep over them, to pray for them, invest time and resource in them and above all to love them in commitment to develop them to their full potential. Training is about task, whereas developing others focuses on character development. True apostolic ministry modeled after Christ raises spiritual sons and daughters. It is noteworthy, that for an effective parent/child relationship to be maintained, the love and authority of the parent must first be wholly accepted by their son or daughter. Thus when a situation arises that needs counsel or discipline, the relationship foundation is firmly in place to allow the parent to administer same. So too, we must face this reality in the Kingdom. If a person is seeking a spiritual mother or father in their lives, they must also be willing to empower this 'parent' to address difficult issues and to accept counsel/discipline as and when necessary. Jesus taught, preached, modeled, encouraged and prayed for all within His sphere of influence. Whether the 3, 12, 72 or thousands Jesus' heart was to sit down amongst the people and make God known. In partnership we ought to seek to emulate the Master in these foundational principles.

Jesus exemplified a lifestyle of love. He occupied, took ground and established the realm of heaven on earth and advanced God's Kingdom. He aligned Himself with His Father's will. As a Man of Faith He was able to release "as it is in heaven … now!" because He partnered with His Father and the Holy Spirit. Godly partnership produces fruit that will last for eternity. Unity is a fruit of partnership and the fruit of unity is the blessing of God on all that we do. God's blessing produces increase and multiplication – life in abundance for all who are in ministry partnership including the masses!

19

～∾

Winning the War vs. Winning the Battle

There will be many battles we face but it is about the full picture. We are to have victory in the war that we as Saints are up against. It is for you to begin today to break through and press on to victory. Don't be deceived. Winning one battle does not mean you've won the war. Until you win your personal battles against fear and any other demon spirits, you're in no shape to get into the real war for other souls.

Wars are made up of many battles. After your first battle is won, you can expect Satan to try to reclaim lost territory by attacking you in three vital areas—your mind, your emotions, and your will.

Remember that Satan is the father of lies. Soon after the victory, he will try to tell you that you were never delivered in the first place. He will try to deceive you by counterfeiting your past symptoms of fear. He will most certainly try to tempt you with the easy way out the next time fear comes along. What do you do? The apostle James instructs us, *"Submit yourselves therefore to God. Resist the devil, and he will flee from you"* (James 4:7).

Now most of us are pretty good at the submission part, and you can submit all you want. But until you fully determine to also resist Satan, there is no fight. When there is no fight, he automatically wins.

However, the moment you choose to stand and resist, you establish a turning point in the war. No longer are you merely Satan's pawn to push around. You are someone to contend with. As soon as you prove to the devil that you mean business, the battle is on.

Therefore put on God's complete armor, that you may be able to resist and stand your ground on the evil day [of danger], and, having done all [the crisis demands], to stand [firmly in your place]. Stand therefore [hold your ground]... (Ephesians 6:13-14 AMP).

Study the entire sixth chapter of Ephesians for yourself. It holds many keys to spiritual warfare, including the armor you must put on for any offensive encounter with the enemy. Any time you stand facing him, holding firm, and exposing the spirit of fear by calling him by name, you are on the offensive!

Of course, you know by now that this kind of warfare is never easy. Jesus battled so hard in the Garden of Gethsemane that He literally sweat blood. If it wasn't easy for Jesus, it won't be easy for you. But the price of not fighting is perpetual immaturity and spiritual stagnation. The writer of Hebrews warned of this when he admonished believers who were falling behind:

You have not yet struggled and fought agonizingly against sin, nor have you resisted and withstood to the point of pouring out your [own] blood (Hebrews 12:4 AMP).

After over 20 years of victorious spiritual warfare, I can tell you that it is at the point when you literally feel (in the spirit) that your own blood is about to be poured out, that God's power sweeps into your being like a flood and the enemy is gone! Is spiritual warfare pretty? No. Will your war against fear be pretty? No. Do you want to grow and be useful to God? Yes! Since you do, God has equipped you with all that you need to do it.

(For the weapons of our warfare are not carnal, but mighty through God to the pulling down of strong holds;) Casting down imaginations, and every high thing that exalteth itself against the knowledge of God, and bringing into captivity every thought to the obedience of Christ (2 Corinthians 10:4-5).

Again, casting down every wayward imagination and bringing every fearful thought to the obedience of Christ will be agonizing at first, but you are not alone. It is all a part of qualifying for God's Army! The apostle Peter described a blow-by-blow account of these spiritual battles (and their outcomes) when he said:

..That enemy of yours, the devil, roams around like a lion roaring [in fierce hunger], seeking someone to seize upon and devour. Withstand him; be firm in faith [against his onset— rooted, established, strong, immovable and determined], knowing that the same (identical) sufferings are appointed to your brotherhood..throughout the world. And after you have suffered a little while, the God of all grace..will Himself complete and make you what you ought to be, establish and ground you securely, and strengthen, and settle you. To Him be the dominion (power, authority, rule) forever and ever. Amen (so be it) (1 Peter 5:8-11 AMP).

The United States has an advance military warning system which warns us if missiles have been fired from an enemy country. If they have, we have only ten minutes to wage a counteroffensive attack against the enemy.

Well, I've got news for you. When that demonic spirit of fear launches one of its "fear missiles" at your mind, you don't have ten minutes to wait. You have one split second in which to decide to counterattack.

This decision takes advance preparation. You must be prepared to instantly choose for the Lord and not against Him. What do I mean? I mean that it is possible to have all of the knowledge of what to do, all the grace of God to do it, all the forces of heaven standing by to help you overcome fear, and still, in that last split second when the enemy roars, you can decide to deny God's power and once again go down to defeat.

The choice is yours. What can you do to get ready to choose Christ in an instant? Have your sword ready!

Let the high praises of God be in their throats and a two-edged sword in their hands (Psalms 149:6 AMP).

Have scriptures that banish fear and praise your Lord ready in your heart and on your tongue. Your sword of the Spirit is the Word of God, fueled by your love for Him. When the enemy looms on the horizon, use your weapons! Speak them. Bind the enemy and defeat him with the Word. Let Christ arise within you. Let His enemies be scattered! You are the victorious one!

Decide right now to put on a new mental attitude toward the battles ahead. Put on a spirit of fierce determination and make up your mind that you will choose to press through every time.

The apostle Paul expressed this same valiant determination when he said:

Not as though I had already attained, either were already perfect: but I follow after, if that I may apprehend that for which also I am apprehended of Christ Jesus. Brethren, I count not myself to have apprehended: but this one thing I do, forgetting those things which are behind, and reaching forth unto those things which are before, I press toward the mark for the prize of the high calling of God in Christ Jesus (Philippians 3:12-14).

Then Paul went on to say, *"Let us therefore, as many as be perfect, be thus minded: and if in any thing ye be otherwise minded, God shall reveal even this unto you"* (Philippians 3:15).

Beloved, one day each one of us, like the servants in the Gospel of Matthew, will stand before our Master and account for every talent He has given to us. But also appearing before the throne of God will be countless souls of our generation, crying out to the Father, *"The harvest is past, the summer is ended, and we are not saved"* (Jeremiah 8:20).

Each year over 120 million people are added to the world's population—unreached and unsaved. How can any one of us, knowing what and whom we have been given, stand by and let any demonic spirit of fear hold us back while millions face eternal death?

The end-time harvest is nearly finished. Countless souls still have not heard the Gospel, and we will be accountable for each one of them. Can you hear God's battle cry in your heart? He is calling to you now, saying:

Have not I commanded you? Be strong, vigorous, and very courageous. Be not afraid, neither be dismayed, for the Lord your God is with you wherever you go (Joshua 1:9 AMP).

Wherever you go, break through, and press on in the mighty Name of Jesus! You are free from fear!

About the Author

Bill Vincent is no stranger to understanding the power of God. Not only has he spent over twenty years as a Minister with a strong prophetic anointing, he is now also an Apostle and Author with Revival Waves of Glory Ministries.

Bill offers a wide range of writings and teachings from deliverance, to experiencing presence of God and developing Apostolic cutting edge Church structure. Drawing on the power of the Holy Spirit through years of experience in Revival and Spiritual Sensitivity. Bill now focuses mainly on pursuing the Presence of God and maintaining Revival.

His books 50 and counting has since helped many people to overcome the spirits and curses of Satan.

Recommended Books

By Bill Vincent
Overcoming Obstacles
Glory: Pursuing God's Presence
Defeating the Demonic Realm
Increasing Your Prophetic Gift
Increase Your Anointing
Keys to Receiving Your Miracle
The Supernatural Realm
Waves of Revival
Increase of Revelation and Restoration
The Resurrection Power of God
Discerning Your Call of God
Apostolic Breakthrough
Glory: Increasing God's Presence
Love is Waiting – Don't Let Love Pass You By
The Healing Power of God
Glory: Expanding God's Presence
Receiving Personal Prophecy
Signs and Wonders
Signs and Wonders Revelations
Children Stories
The Rapture
The Secret Place of God's Power
Building a Prototype Church

Breakthrough of Spiritual Strongholds
Glory: Revival Presence of God
Overcoming the Power of Lust
Glory: Kingdom Presence of God
Transitioning to the Prototype Church
The Stronghold of Jezebel
Healing After Divorce
A Closer Relationship With God
Cover Up and Save Yourself
Desperate for God's Presence
The War for Spiritual Battles
Spiritual Leadership
Global Warning
Millions of Churches
Destroying the Jezebel Spirit
Awakening of Miracles
Deception and Consequences Revealed
Are You a Follower of Christ
Don't Let the Enemy Steal from You!
A Godly Shaking
The Unsearchable Riches of Christ
Heaven's Court System
Satan's Open Doors
Armed for Battle
The Wrestler
Spiritual Warfare: Complete Collection
Growing In the Prophetic
Faith
The Angry Fighter's Story
Understanding Heaven's Court System
Restoration of the Soul
Spiritual Warfare Made Simple
Aligning With God's Promises

Deep Hunger
Beginning the Courts of Heaven
Breaking Curses
Writing and Publishing a Book
How to Write a Book
The Anointing
The Courts of Heaven

Web Site:
www.revivalwavesofgloryministries.com

CPSIA information can be obtained
at www.ICGtesting.com
Printed in the USA
LVHW020356110220
646447LV00013B/460/J